Religions and Religious Movements
HINDUISM

Jeff Hay, Book Editor

Bruce Glassman, Vice President

Bonnie Szumski, Publisher, Series Editor

Helen Cothran, Managing Editor

GREENHAVEN PRESS
An imprint of Thomson Gale, a part of The Thomson Corporation

THOMSON
✳ ™
GALE

Detroit • New York • San Francisco • San Diego • New Haven, Conn.
Waterville, Maine • London • Munich

THOMSON

GALE

™

LIBRARY OF CONGRESS CATALOGING-IN-PUBLICATION DATA

Hinduism / Jeff Hay, book editor.
   p. cm. — (Religions and religious movements)
Includes bibliographical references and index.
ISBN 0-7377-2569-9 (lib. : alk. paper)
   1. Hinduism—History. 2. God (Hinduism). 3. India—Religious life and customs.
4. India—Civilization. I. Hay, Jeff. II. Series.
BL1150.H46 2006
294.5'09—dc22

2004052325

Printed in the United States of America

Contents

years, from 1757 to 1947, inspired various Hindu reform and nationalist movements.

Foreword

"Religion is not what is grasped by the brain, but a heart grasp."
—Mohandas Gandhi, 1956

The impulse toward religion—to move beyond the world as we know it and ponder the larger questions of why we are here, whether there is a God who directs our lives, and how we should live—seems as universally human as breathing.

Yet, although this impulse is universal, different religions and their adherents are often at odds due to conflicts that stem from their opposing belief systems. These conflicts can also occur because many people have only the most tentative understanding of religions other than their own. In a time when religion seems to be at the root of growing tensions around the world, its study seems particularly relevant.

We live in a religiously diverse world. And while the world's many religions have coexisted for millennia, only recently, with information shared so easily and travel to even the most remote regions made possible for larger numbers of people, has this fact been fully acknowledged. It is no longer possible to ignore other religions, regardless of whether one views these religions positively or negatively.

The study of religion has also changed a great deal in recent times. Just a few decades ago in the United States, few students were exposed to any religion other than Christianity. Today, the study of religion reflects the pluralism of American society and the world at large. Religion courses and even current events classes focus on non-Christian religions as well as the religious experiences of groups that have in the past been marginalized by traditional Christianity, such as women and racial minorities.

In fact, the study of religion has been integrated into many different types of classes and disciplines. Anthropology, psychology, sociology, history, philosophy, political science, economics, and other fields often include discussions about different nations' religions and beliefs.

The study of religion involves so many disciplines because, for many cultures, it is integrated into many different parts of life. This point is often highlighted when American companies conduct business deals in Middle Eastern countries and inadvertently offend a host country's religious constrictions, for example. On both a small scale, such as personal travel, and on a large scale, such as international trade and politics, an understanding of the world's religions has become essential.

The goals of the Religions and Religious Movements series are several. The first is to provide students a historical context for each of the world's religions. Each book focuses on one religion and explores, through primary and secondary sources, its fundamental belief system, religious works of importance, and prominent figures. By using articles from a variety of sources, each book provides students with different theological and historical contexts for the religion.

The second goal of the series is to explore the challenges that each religion faces today. All of these religions are experiencing challenges and changes—some theological, some political—that are forcing alterations in attitude and belief. By reading about these current dilemmas, students will come to understand that religions are not abstract concepts, but a vital part of peoples' lives.

The last and perhaps most important objective is to make students aware of the wide variety of religious beliefs, as well as the factors, common to all religions. Every religion attempts to puzzle out essential questions as well as provide a model for doing good in the world. By using the books in the Religions and Religious Movements series, students will find that people with divergent, closely held beliefs may learn to live together and work toward the same goals.

Introduction

Karma. Dharma. Reincarnation. Hare Krishnas. Mantras. *Kama Sutra.* These words or phrases are familiar to many modern Americans. They are connected to Hinduism, one of the great world religions and, according to most experts, the oldest. Although Hinduism is most closely associated with India, since the 1850s Hinduism has become a growing religion in Western nations such as Great Britain, Canada, Australia, and even the United States. The increasing presence of Hindus in the West has greatly increased awareness of Hinduism outside India. Meanwhile, satellites, the Internet, and other technological tools have made the world more closely connected. India and Indians have begun to play larger roles in the world, and thus the need to understand this ancient faith has increased as well.

Hinduism's development began, most experts believe, with certain religious practices of the oldest known civilization in India, the Indus Valley civilization based in modern-day Pakistan and northwest India, which arose sometime around 2800 B.C. Archaeological evidence suggests that the Indus Valley people may have worshipped an early mother goddess who later reappeared in such Hindu forms as Kali, Durga, and Parvati. They may also have worshipped an early version of Shiva, one of the most important Hindu gods, and practiced ritual bathing, a characteristic of Hinduism even today. The fact that Indus Valley writing has yet to be deciphered by archaeologists, however, limits definitive knowledge of this civilization. Even the decline of the Indus Valley civilization in the centuries after 2000 B.C. has yet to be fully explained. Many experts argue, however, that even though Indus Valley people deserted their cities and migrated to other parts of India, they likely kept some of their gods and religious customs.

The First Wave of Migrants

A major wave of migrations into India began sometime around 1200 B.C. Although little is known about these migrants, scholars think they were members of the Indo-Aryan tribe that originated in the Caucasus region of southwestern Asia. These warlike newcomers established political and military domination over the more docile native inhabitants of India. Inevitably, however, the two groups integrated, and it was this integration that created Indian civilization and the Hindu religion.

The Indo-Aryans brought with them both their gods and their religious texts. These gods included Indra, a warlike god of fire; Varuna, the god of universal order; and even an early version of Krishna. The texts included the Vedas, four collections of chants, hymns, and rituals whose importance to ancient India was so clear that historians refer to the centuries from 1200 to 800 B.C. as the Vedic age. The Rig-Veda is the main one of the four, the oldest accepted text in Hinduism. It was written in Sanskrit, an ancient religious language still used by Hindu teachers and holy persons, and may have been passed down through oral tradition—via memorization and recitation—for centuries. Other religious texts, such as the Upanishads, established the personal aspects of Hindu belief by emphasizing lessons between a guru, or teacher, and his disciple.

India's caste system also developed as a result of the integration of the Aryan newcomers with native inhabitants. It seems to have emerged as an early form of racial segregation, as the Sanskrit word for caste, *varna*, also means "color." The Aryans who dominated India may have wanted to remain both separate from the darker-skinned locals and to reserve the highest positions in society—and therefore the highest status—for themselves. Indian society during the Vedic age was divided into four basic castes, and these distinctions remained in place for centuries. The highest caste was the Brahman, or priestly, caste. Next highest were the Kshatriya, or warriors and rulers. Third was the Vaisya, or productive, caste, made up of landowners and craftspersons. The lowest caste was the Shudra, or laboring, caste; as Indian society and economy developed, the Shudra caste was further divided into subcastes based on specific jobs. Meanwhile, a fifth group of so-called untouchables, who were technically outcastes, was added to the system. The untouchables, whom in the twentieth century Mahatma Gandhi renamed the *harijans*, or "children of god," performed the dirtiest jobs, such as sweeping and dealing with dead bodies. In the beginning the top three castes were reserved for the Aryans while the indigenous inhabitants of India were either relegated to the Shudra caste or were turned into untouchables.

The Caste System and Hinduism

During the centuries after 1000 B.C. the caste system became closely connected with evolving Hindu beliefs, and the religion has therefore served to reinforce caste ideas. Hindus believe in reincarnation, or the transmigration of souls. In other words, the soul is eternal, and over different lifetimes it inhabits many different bodies. Gurus began to teach, moreover, that the ultimate goal of the individual soul is to rejoin Brahman, or the oversoul, the single, divine godhead. This process is known as *moksha*, the release from the wheel of birth and death. Only Brahman-caste Hindus can achieve *moksha*, and even they may face rebirth many more times. Members of the other castes are even farther away from *moksha*, with the untouchables the farthest away of all.

Hindus therefore attempt to live their lives in a manner that will allow them to attain or at least move closer to *moksha*. They try to follow their dharma, a word that has several meanings in Hinduism but that here is perhaps best translated as "duty." Each person has many dharmas. Some are connected with daily life, such as proper marriage and devotion to family. Other duties are religious. High-caste Hindus, for instance, must have sons so that those sons can light the fires on their fathers' funeral pyres to ensure that their fathers' souls are reborn closer to *moksha*. Certain Brahmans are raised to perform rituals intended to help maintain cosmic order. Indeed, the higher one stands in the caste system, the higher the expectations are of one. Meanwhile, the failure to fulfill one's dharma may result in the piling up of bad karma, a term that indicates that all actions have moral consequences. Too much bad karma may result in one's soul being born farther away from *moksha*. It is not possible in Hinduism to accumulate good karma by doing good deeds. Good behavior is simply expected as a part of one's dharma.

Two Great Epic Poems

Hindu concepts such as *moksha*, dharma, and karma are reinforced in a number of texts that appeared during the period from approximately 800 B.C. to A.D. 200. Prominent among them are the great epic poems the *Mahabharata* and the *Ramayana*. The *Ramayana* emphasizes the importance of staying true to one's duties in the face of rivals and evil temptations by using the examples of the god Rama, the ideal king and husband, and his consort, Sita, the ideal wife. The *Mahabharata*, meanwhile, takes place in the years of the Aryan settlement of northern India. One of its great episodes is the Bhagavad Gita, in which the god Krishna reminds Arjuna, a Kshatriya-caste Hindu, of the importance of following his warrior's dharma in the face of his many misgivings. The Bhagavad Gita remains, perhaps, the most central and popular Hindu text.

Other texts further refined Hinduism. Among the most important is the Laws of Manu, attributed to a likely fictional Hindu sage known as Manu. The Laws of Manu discusses how Hindus might address practical issues of law and custom in daily life. Other guidebooks include the Artha Shastra, which is concerned with acquiring and maintaining wealth, power, and position; and the Kama Sutra, a manual of love, sex, and etiquette directed at upper-class young men. These two texts are reflections of what Hindu experts have argued are the three goals of life: pleasure (*kama*), power (*artha*), and religious devotion. According to Hinduism, these three goals should be balanced, with no one goal becoming more important than the others. The goals roughly reflect the Hindu man's four stages of life: student, householder, retiree and devotee, and finally, ascetic and holy man. During the first of these stages, the student's stage, a focus on *kama*, or pleasure, is to be expected. During the second, the householder stage when one is a husband, father, and working productively, the proper goal is *artha*, broadly defined as not only political power but the search for wealth and position. During the third stage, once one's children are grown, one's focus shifts to religious devotion. The fourth of these stages, the life of a wandering religious ascetic, is reached by few Hindus, but nevertheless this group is for men who leave worldly life behind, forsaking all possessions and comfort, and devoting their entire lives to meditation and worship. These men are worthy of great respect in Hindu India.

As Hinduism evolved and developed, it also began to produce offshoots. A few have been different enough and large enough to achieve status as separate religions. Most prominent among them is Buddhism, which was begun by a Kshatriya-caste prince turned religious teacher during the sixth century B.C. Buddhism was turned into a major religion by the converted Indian king Ashoka during the fourth century B.C. Another major variation from the same era was Jainism, which was established by a saint known as Mahavira. Jains believe in strict vegetarianism and nonviolence and help reinforce in Hinduism the symbol of the river as a method to purify the soul.

Meanwhile, during the first millennium A.D. Hinduism spread from India to Southeast Asia, where it had a major impact on emerging empires in areas as far away as Cambodia and the islands of Indonesia. Taken to these regions first by merchants and traveling holy men, and adopted by kings and tribal chieftains seeking to gain trade or military advantages, Hinduism played an important role in the development of advanced civilizations in Southeast Asia. Most of those areas converted, in time, to either Buddhism or Islam. But these newer arrivals simply overlaid Hinduism (as

Ganesha, the elephant-headed Hindu god, is known as the remover of obstacles, the god of domestic harmony, and of success.

well as even earlier religions), and Hindu influence can be seen in such famous monuments as Angkor Wat in Cambodia. Only one place outside India today, the Indonesian island of Bali, continues to practice Hinduism as its major faith. Balinese society is divided into castes, and local versions of Vishnu and Shiva are worshipped in a complex variety of ceremonies.

A Religion of Many Gods

As Hinduism's openness and flexibility produced new religions, and as it spread to regions outside India, a large and colorful pantheon of gods emerged and became central to the daily practice and common understanding of the faith. There are hundreds, or even thousands, of Hindu gods, depending on the source consulted, but a number of them have emerged as the most lasting in the centuries after A.D. 200. First and foremost is the great trinity of Brahma, the creator of the universe; Shiva, the creator and destroyer of life; and Vishnu, the preserver of life. Shiva and Vishnu remain the most popular of the gods, versions of them have been worshipped perhaps as early as the first two millennia B.C. Indeed, one of the two dominant schools of Hinduism that emerged during the first millennium B.C., the theistic school, emphasizes the worship of either Shiva or Vishnu. For Shaivites, who worship Shiva, and for Vaishnavites, who worship Vishnu, these gods have become the center of their faith and the focus of their devotion. Other Hindus worship aspects of Shiva, personified as gods such as Ganesha or Hanuman, or even Shiva's consorts: goddesses such as Saraswathi or the female trinity of Kali/Durga/Parvati, a deity in which many Hindus find aspects of the female side of creation.

Vishnu, meanwhile, is often worshipped in the form of one of his nine known avatars, or incarnations. The most popular of these are Rama and Krishna, but another is Siddhartha Gautama, the founder of Buddhism. Beyond this main group are innumerable other gods, and new ones are created constantly when earlier ones fall out of favor. For Hindus, worship of one god or goddess primarily has to do with local tradition and custom or with one's immediate circumstances—such as if someone is facing a drought, an epidemic, or the possibility of wealth—rather than with a sense that one god or goddess is "truer" or "better" than any other. All devotion and worship reach, ultimately, back to the one universal and timeless godhead, which makes its presence among humans known by taking many forms and using many different names. This emphasis in Hinduism is the basis of the second major school, absolutism. Absolutists focus on trying to reach the divine as closely and personally as possible—understanding that all people carry a piece of the divine within— rather than emphasizing the worship and attributes of this or that god.

Invaders and a Foreign Faith

Absolutism, ironically, was reinforced by India's largest wave of invaders and migrants since the Indo-Aryans centuries earlier: the Muslims. Muslim traders had begun to settle in India not long after the rise of Islam in the Middle East during the seventh century. But Islam only became a major force in India after the arrival of Persian-speaking Turkish conquerors during the 1100s and 1200s. Indeed, much of northern India was under the control of various Muslim rulers from 1206, when the regime known as the Delhi Sultanate came to power, until 1757, when the Mogul Empire ceased to be a dominant power. Muslims found India a fertile field for conversion; many among the lower castes, as well as the untouchables, found they could be free of caste restrictions by converting to Islam. Even kings and other powerful leaders converted to Islam to gain political or economic advantages.

Religious thinkers from both Hinduism and Islam tried to reconcile the two faiths, but with little success. One major result of this effort, however, was the bhakti, or devotional, tradition of Hinduism, which thrived during much of the Muslim period. Like the Sufi branch of Islam, bhakti Hinduism emphasized personal devotion to and connection with God, and it produced some of the greatest Hindu poetry, thereby adding to an ongoing canon of great Hindu texts dating back to the Vedas. Some of the bhakti poets, such as Kabir, writing during the 1500s and early 1600s, took an extreme version of the absolutist line, claiming that theistic Hindus were too preoccupied with gods, rituals, and obscure teachings to really "see" God, while Muslims were much the same. In many of his poems, however, Kabir refers to God as "Ram" or "Rama," one of the many names from the Hindu pantheon. Other great bhakti poets and teachers included Mirabai and Chaitanya.

The bhakti tradition, along with the challenge of Islam, produced in turn a new Indian religion: Sikhism. Founded by Guru Nanak during the sixteenth century and practiced by millions in India and around the world today, Sikhism serves as a sort of third alternative between Hinduism and Islam with its emphasis on the oneness of God; the importance of gurus, or teachers; and the necessity of a fairly strict code of behavior.

Despite their long political control over much of India, and despite a substantial number of converts, Muslim rulers had little impact on the majority of Indians, who lived as their ancestors always had in the country's innumerable small villages. Of probably greater impact on most Hindus was the most recent wave of foreign rulers and migrants, the British, who brought with them modern industrial technology, the railroad and telegraph, new economic forms, beliefs in universal education and democratic politics, and, perhaps most importantly, the English language. These provided yet another set of influences to be digested and absorbed by Hindus.

English merchants established trading posts in India in the early 1600s. By 1757 the English began taking over territory until, by the early 1800s, they were the dominant power in India. They remained in charge until India's independence in 1947.

Ironically these foreigners from faraway Europe added an element to Hinduism that had been lacking: a sense of its own history. In the late 1700s and early 1800s a group of British scholars known as Orientalists learned Sanskrit and the other major Indian languages and began to trace the historical evolution of Hinduism. It was they, for instance, who first argued that Indo-Aryan migrants played a role in the foundation of the religion and that, even more surprisingly to many, the Indo-Aryans may have been related to tribal groups that helped to settle Europe during the second millennium B.C. They also assembled a collection of canonical, or central, Hindu texts and gave the religion a name: Hinduism, a term that really means little more than "Indianism." This desire to write "Hindu history" was unknown to most Hindus, who accepted that their religion was timeless and that the gods operated according to their own schedule, which lay largely beyond human understanding. Also, since religious beliefs were so intertwined with daily life, Hindus had no real need to name their religion aside from the use of the Sanskrit term *sanatana dharma*, or "the one way."

British-influenced Hindu reformers began to appear in the early 1800s. One was Ram Mohan Roy (1772–1833), who came from the province of Bengal, where the British capital of Calcutta lay. Heavily influenced by Islam, by Protestant Christianity, and by his travels in England, Roy came to believe that much of the ritualism, caste restrictions, and gods in Hinduism were unnecessary, and he tried to emphasize the rational and humanistic aspects of the faith. Among his more memorable efforts was to try to explain to Hindus why the British were correct in seeking to abolish the practice of suttee, in which devout Hindu wives were expected to join their dead husbands on their funeral pyres. Other reformers who worked to reconcile Hindu traditions with the West were Ramakrishna (1836–1886) and Vivekenanda (1863–1902), who established institutions to perform outreach and good works in both India and around the world, many of which still exist. Another strand of Hindu reform groups, meanwhile, focused their efforts on both trying to protect their ancient faith from outside "threats" such as the British, and on taking steps to end British rule altogether.

Mahatma Gandhi and Modern India

When the British, exhausted and impoverished by World War II, decided to leave India in 1947, they made a fateful decision: to partition India into two nations. One, India proper, would be dominated by Hindu elites. The other, Pakistan, would protect the interests of the region's millions of Muslims. The decision for partition was much opposed by a man who had worked hard to establish India's independence and revive Hindu religious life. This was Mahatma Gandhi, the most recognizable of all Hindu leaders during the twentieth century. Born Mohandas K. Gandhi to a Vaisya-caste family in western India, Gandhi was trained as a lawyer in London and worked among Indian expatriates in South Africa before taking up the nationalist cause. Gandhi used the Bhagavad Gita as his chief spiritual guide, and from it he adapted the principle of detached action to his efforts to oust British rule. He concluded that nonviolent resistance would establish the moral superiority of his cause, and he spent much of the 1920s and 1930s in demonstrations as well as in British prisons. Gandhi was not only interested in politics, however. He rejected the modern, industrialized world as soulless, preached the equality of all religions, and tried to raise the social level of the lowest class in India, the untouchables, whom he took to his heart. In the early 1940s, after communal riots among Hindus, Muslims, and Sikhs broke out, which in time were to kill hundreds of thousands, Gandhi was heartbroken at the turn toward religious violence. In early 1948 he was killed by a conspiracy of Hindu fundamentalists, who apparently found his teachings far too radical. This simple man, who for years had strode across India clad in nothing more than a loincloth of his own weaving, came to be considered a mahatma, or "great soul," by most Hindus, and he continues to be revered.

Modern democratic India, which now is populated by more than 1 billion people, is officially a secular state in which religion and caste are supposed to play only a very small part in public life. Traditions thousands of years old do not fade easily, however, and numerous tensions based on religion have continued to trouble Indians. Movements to grant special privileges such as government jobs and university spots to low-caste Hindus and untouchables have inspired a reaction that reaches its extreme in a broad Hindu fundamentalist movement, which claims its own national political party, the Bharatiya Janata Party. In the nation's hundreds of thousands of rural villages, meanwhile, the modern world has made little impact, and people continue to be oppressed and exploited if they belong to society's lower orders, while Brahmans continue to claim their privileges and their high religious status. In India's big cities—including Mumbai (Bombay), Kolkata (Calcutta), and Delhi, some of the largest cities on earth—a rising middle class has become increasingly secular in its way of life, and for many residents, Hindu traditions provide little more than a picturesque past and an excuse for holidays. And over it all is the continual threat of religious violence, especially between Hindu fundamentalists who demand a religiously pure state and the nation's Muslims, who, despite partition, still number some 150 million.

Meanwhile, the migrations of Hindus around the world over the last 150 years have turned Hinduism into a truly global faith; according to some accounts, communities of nonresident Indians are even more devout than their counterparts in India, especially in the rich countries of the West. In any case, as the world is drawn closer together, one can see the testing of what may be one of the most basic of Hindu ideas: that all humanity, and indeed all creation, is connected, that the world is best described as unity in diversity.

CHAPTER 1

The Origins of Hinduism

Archaeologists Believe Religious Images from Ancient India Are Precursors of Hinduism

by Bridget and Raymond Allchin

In the following selection British archaeologists Bridget and Raymond Allchin examine relics of the earliest known civilization in India and find that certain of its artistic motifs suggest connections with later aspects of Hinduism. This early civilization, known variously as the Indus, Indus Valley, or Harappan civilization, and usually dated sometime from 2800 B.C. to 1800 B.C., remains mysterious. Its ruins were discovered only in the 1920s, leaving little time for archaeological examination in the decades since. Furthermore, its written language has yet to be deciphered. Experts, therefore, can only speculate on Indus Valley religious beliefs based on images left on walls and seals, on statues and other images, on the remains of temples, and on the contents of grave sites.

Using these sources the Allchins find a number of common features between the religious customs of the Indus Valley civilization and later, more developed Hindu practices. These include early versions of the Mother Goddess, later found in such deities as Kali and

Durga, and even of Shiva, one of the most revered Hindu gods. Bridget Allchin taught archaeology at Cambridge University in the United Kingdom, while Raymond Allchin was a lecturer in Indian Studies at Cambridge.

In spite of the mystery of its undeciphered inscriptions, there is still a considerable body of information concerning the religion of the Indus civilization. A number of buildings both on the citadel [central fortress] and in the lower town at Mohenjodaro have been tentatively identified as temples. It is from these that a part of the small repertoire of stone sculptures, almost certainly all cult icons, derive. But our information goes far beyond. [In the 1930s archaeologist] Sir John Marshall, in his brilliant [writings] upon the religion of the Indus civilization, was able to propose certain basic elements. He concluded that the great numbers of female terra-cotta figurines were popular representations of the Great Mother Goddess; and he rightly drew parallels between this evidence and the ubiquitous cult of goddesses both throughout modern India and in literature. He further postulated the presence of a great male God, whom he identified with the later [Shiva], and who shared many of his epithets. We are of the opinion that the stone cult icons, and therefore probably also the temples, were dedicated to this same deity. One of the most significant representations is to be found on a series of seals. These show him seated in a Yogic [meditation] posture, upon a low throne flanked by antelopes, and wearing a great horned headdress, he is ithyphallic [has an erect penis], he has perhaps three faces, and he is surrounded by jungle creatures. Every one of these features can be found in the descriptions of [Shiva] of later times. Moreover, stones identical in form to the *lingam*, the phallic emblem of [Shiva], were found in the cities.

Another group of human figures on seals and amulets, whether male or female, have horns on the head and long tails; they sometimes also have the hind legs and hoofs of cattle. From the seals, seal impressions, amulets and copper tablets, we may derive a series of items which must belong to the religious ideology of the Harappans. On one seal rearing cobras accompany the Yogi figure. A recurrent theme is of a tree-spirit, of indeterminate sex, shown in a tree, with a tiger or other animal standing before it. This motif is occasionally combined with a pair of worshippers bearing rooted plants or saplings. Another theme shows a row of seven figures, also of uncertain sex, with long hair plaits, standing before a tree, or tree with spirit. The seven have been variously identified with the seven Rishis (or seers), and with the seven Mothers of later times. Some scenes are strongly suggestive of Mesopotamian mythology: for example, a man grappling with a pair of tigers recalls the Gilgamesh motif, and the horned god, with the legs and tail of a bull, recalls the Bull-man Enkidu of the same epic [the *Epic of Gilgamesh*]. Wild and domestic animals are also commonly depicted. Many of these are naturalistic representations, and the extent of their religious significance is not clear, although the bull and cow may be expected to have had a special role comparable with that of later times. We need have no doubt in assigning such a role to the composite animals, such as the creature with the forepart of a human and the hindquarters of a tiger—perhaps the ancestor of the Tiger Mother of modern south India—or the composite Bull-elephant, the Ram-bull-elephant, and so on. The last has been compared by [scholars H.] Mode and [D.D.] Kosambi with a similar beast from Jemdet-Nasr [in Mesopotamia]. It also demands comparison with compound creatures, such as the Lion-elephant of folk-tales and medieval iconography. Even abstract symbols and motifs seem to anticipate later Indian religion. Among these we may note the maze-like closed patterns which recall the auspicious rice-flour designs made by housewives upon thresholds or in courtyards; the *svastika* in several variant forms; and the *pīpal* leaf.

Evidence from Grave Sites

There is a definite division between graveyard and city, although it is not clear whether burials were discovered within the city in the earlier excavations. The dominant mode of disposal was extended inhumation [buried lying down], and only in Cemetery H at Harappa was a new practice, the placing of collected, disarticulated [unassembled] bones in large urns, in evidence.

The burials of Cemetery H at Harappa are of importance for more than one reason. In the lower of the two strata they were predominantly inhumations with grave goods. The pottery of some (which we may suppose to have been the earliest in time) is reported to resemble that 'of the mounds', that is to say of the main Harappan occupation. In other cases the pottery introduces both new forms and new painted patterns, which as we have already noticed recall those of sites in Iran. In the upper Stratum we find the new, and probably intrusive rite of burying bones with other goods in large urns. The painted urns tell us all that is so far known of the beliefs of their makers. On their shoulders these urns bear registers bounded by straight or wavy lines. Common motifs are peacocks, with long streaming feathers on the head. In one case their bodies are hollow and contain small horizontal human forms. A second motif is of bulls or cows, some with curious plant-like forms springing from their horns, one with a *pīpal* leaf appearing from the hump. Another shows two beasts facing each other, held by a man with long wavy hair, while a hound stands menacingly behind one of them; in yet another a little man of similar form stands on the back of a creature which shares the features of a centaur with the Harappan Bull-man. Other painted designs are mainly natural: stars, leaves, trees, etc. [Indus Valley archaeologist Nadhu Sarup] Vats suggested that the tiny human forms within the peacock are the souls of the dead; that the broad registers represent the river across which they must be carried, and that the peacocks, bulls and so forth are other aids to their crossing. In support of this he quoted possibly related extracts from the Rigveda [Hindu scripture]. Perhaps the most convincing detail is the hound, which he compares with the hound of Yama, the [Hindu] god of death. Thus in this pottery we may find a striking combination of Harappan elements, such as the *pīpal* leaf, the bull, and perhaps the peacock, with a use and conception which seem foreign. It is indeed tempting to see in this material evidence of an intrusion of an early wave of Indo-Iranians, perhaps related to the authors of the Rigveda.

Hinduism's Disputed Beginnings

by Kim Knott

Hinduism, the oldest of the major world religions, has mysterious origins that remain a subject of dispute among believers and religious scholars. Most agree that Hinduism first developed during the period when migrants from Central Asia, known variously as Indo-Europeans, Indo-Aryans, or simply Aryans (after *arya*, a word meaning "land of the blessed or noble"), entered India during the second millennium B.C. There they merged with earlier inhabitants of the Indian subcontinent, whose influence on Aryan religion, some claim, was substantial. These earlier inhabitants may have been the descendants of those who built the so-called Indus Valley civilization in northwestern India in the third millennium B.C. and whose religious practices involved meditation, ritual bathing, and perhaps even worship of an early version of the great Hindu god Shiva. In any case the Aryan migrants emerged as the dominant group, and the earliest accepted Hindu scriptures, the Vedas, were in Sanskrit, an Aryan language.

In the following selection, religious scholar Kim Knott examines various schools of thought concerning the origins of Hinduism, including the one that claims that, since Hindu beliefs are timeless, they cannot really be said to have an origin. She notes also that much of the modern world's understanding of early Hinduism comes from the work of scholars active during the years when Great Britain controlled India (1757–1947), implying that this search for origins is a relatively recent point of concern for Hindus. Kim Knott is head of the Department of Theology and Religious Studies at the University of Leeds in the United Kingdom.

How do Hindus understand their origins and the early formation of their religion? Many describe Hinduism as *sanatana dharma*, the eternal tradition or religion. This refers to the idea that its origins lie beyond human history, and its truths have been divinely revealed . . . and passed down through the ages to the present day in the most ancient of the world's scriptures, the *Veda*. Many share this faith perspective, but various differing views arise when it comes to interpreting human history in early India. A popular view today among some Hindus—particularly those who are often referred to as Hindu nationalists, owing to their belief that Hinduism is India's true religion—is that divine truth was revealed to the Aryans, whom they see as the noble, enlightened race which lived in India thousands of years ago. The Aryans shared a great language, Sanskrit, in which the Vedic scriptures were composed, and built a majestic Hindu civilization, the rituals, literature, and law of which remain the common culture of Hindus today and India's rightful national heritage. According to this view, people belonging to the religions which developed in India after the time of the Aryans, like Buddhists, Jains, and Sikhs, are all embraced as part of the

Hindu religion. But many Hindus, as well as Buddhists, Jains, and Sikhs themselves, do not share this understanding. They challenge the idea that the roots of Hinduism were entirely Aryan. They believe instead that some of the great deities and important religious developments that we now associate with Hinduism came from indigenous people who lived in India before the Aryans. According to them, the latter were incomers, migrating into north-west India, conquering peaceful, settled communities, imposing their ideology yet absorbing what was valuable and popular from the surrounding culture. This has also been a widely held view among Western scholars, who have dated the Aryan migration to about 1500 BCE and the *Rig Veda*, the earliest known scripture of the Aryans, to about 1200 BCE.

Differing Views of Hinduism's Beginnings

In addition to those who hold one of these two broad views, there are many other Hindus whose reconstruction of early Indian history derives from the particular teachings of the Hindu group or sect to which they belong. In short, there is no single devotional perspective. Equally, scholars have differing views. The material evidence, from archaeological remains and early texts, does not provide a clear picture, and many questions remain unanswered for devotees and scholars alike.

Earlier this century, for example, British and Indian archaeologists uncovered the remains of several early cities in what was then north India (now Pakistan) which they dated to 2500–1800 BCE, a period before the time when Aryan migrants were thought to have entered north-west India. The society and culture attributed to these cities is now referred to as the Indus val-

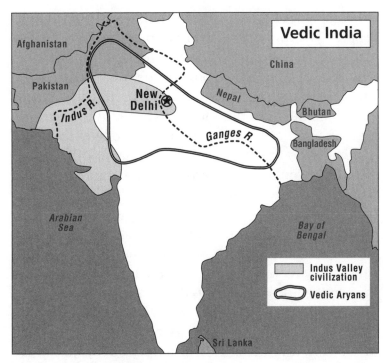

ley civilization (denoting its location) or the Harappan civilization (Harappa being one of the two major cities, Mohenjo-daro being the other). The religion of these cities involved temple rites, fertility rituals, the use of animals, perhaps for sacrifice, and ritual bathing in a large pool constructed of stone. Tiles or seals have been found depicting an as yet undeciphered script and religious symbols of various kinds.

Is the seated, horned figure surrounded by animals found on one seal an early depiction of the god Shiva? Are the many female figurines found in the cities and neighbouring villages merely fertility symbols, or are they evidence of a form of goddess worship which has continued unabated throughout the centuries and is still found today? Is the Indus script an early relative of Sanskrit and thus an Indo-European language, or is it a Dravidian language spoken and written by early indigenous people? Was the urban civilization of the Indus valley surpassed by the pastoral society and culture of Aryan migrants, or were all or some of the inhabitants of the cities of Harappa and Mohenjo-daro themselves Aryan?

Indian and Western indologists are actively researching these and other questions in the hope of shedding more light on the early history of India. Another group of Indian scholars uses astronomical data and calculations to date events mentioned in early texts. But how interested people—whether scholars or devotees—then interpret their new information and ideas is not a simple matter. They often have theories of their own into which they fit such new data. Scholars often claim that they are guided solely by the available evidence in drawing their conclusions, but we need only to look back to the early scholarly work by Westerners in India to see how the ideological interests of the time may have affected their work.

An Important Western Interpretation

Most of the eighteenth- and early nineteenth-century scholars (we often refer to them as 'orientalists') who first undertook the translation of Sanskrit texts and the reconstruction of the Aryan past were also British administrators. In this capacity, they needed to acquire a good understanding of Hindu culture and traditions in order to help in the establishment of British colonial rule in India. Inspired by what they learnt about the similarities between Sanskrit and European languages and about the Aryan people described in the Sanskrit texts, some of them drew conclusions about the common origins of Indo-European societies and cultures.

The romantic view which they put forward was appealing to some people in Europe and India because it suggested a common descent from noble (*aryan*) origins. With its roots in early Western scholarship, it was this view, of a great Aryan race and civilization, that later became popular with Hindu nationalists. The leaders of a late nineteenth-century Hindu movement called the Arya Samaj were among the first to look back to such a golden age and to claim a continuous, unified history for selected Hindu beliefs, values, and practices from that time. What had originally been a colonial scholarly perspective was taken up by this and other groups whose religious and political views it matched.

There is a great desire among many Indians and those who study India to understand her past and to resolve these difficult questions. But it is not just a matter of uncovering more historical information in order to complete the jigsaw. It is often the case that new discoveries, while answering some questions, throw up other ones. A complete picture rarely emerges at all, and there is always room for further speculation and hypothesis. What is more, devotional understandings of early history follow their own rules, not those of scholarly evidence and argument. They are guided first and foremost by revelation. Where historical evidence can support a devotional view, it may be welcomed, but a firm religious conviction does not require such evidence in order to thrive. It depends rather on faith. For some Hindus, then, all this argument about what happened in early India is only relevant where it accords with what the scriptures tell them. However, as we have seen, there are plenty of modern Hindus who feel strongly that scholarly theories and historical data offer important support for what they believe.

Ancient Aryan Migrants to India and Their Religion

by Stanley Wolpert

Most experts agree that Hinduism, like Indian civilization in general, is the result of the influences of two cultures: the so-called Dravidian peoples, who were among the original inhabitants of the subcontinent and who may have been the descendants of the mysterious Indus Valley civilization of approximately 2800–1800 B.C., and the so-called Indo-Europeans, or Aryans, migrants from southwestern Asia who entered India sometime between 2000 and 1000 B.C. In the following selection Stanley Wolpert, professor of Indian history at the University of California, Los Angeles, describes the religion practiced by these ancient Aryans and suggests certain possible influences that their beliefs had on the later development of Hinduism. His main resource is the Rig-Veda, the earliest of the texts considered central to Hinduism. Wolpert's reliance on the Rig-Veda points to one of the major problems in understanding ancient Hinduism and ancient India: the lack of reliable written historical resources beyond the Rig-Veda itself.

―――――――――――――

The religion of the early Aryans centered around the worship of a pantheon of nature gods, to whom sacrificial offerings were periodically made for the good things of life and for repose thereafter. No one deity ruled over the pantheon, which included some thirty-three divinities named in the Rig Veda, but the most powerful gods, to whom many hymns were addressed, were Indra, Varuna, Agni, and Soma. Indra was the war god, youthful, heroic, ever victorious. Like [the Norse god] Thor, he wields thunderbolts and hovers in atmospheric realms, assisted by an obscure storm god named Rudra, who comes to be identified only much later as the Rig Vedic form of Shiva. The association of Indra with the power to release waters as well as win wars helps explain his special significance, for he is hailed as "surpassing floods and rivers in his greatness." Perhaps he was the first great leader of the Aryan conquest, a historic figure whose youthful force overcame all obstacles, standing so tall and strong he seemed to hold Father Sky upon his shoulders, separating it from Mother Earth, as one simplistic myth of Vedic creation insisted. He required much nourishment and drank his *soma* [a drink thought to increase bravery] greedily in three gulps every morning before going forth to defeat the demon Vritra, whose limbless body enclosed all creation, including the sun, waters, and cows, holding life in a state of inert suspension and darkness. With his "mighty and fatal weapon," the thunderbolt, Indra pierced the dark demon's covering and released the dawn (which is why Hindu prayers to Indra are chanted so early every morning, to help him defeat the night), leaving the demon "prostrate" while the waters, "like bellowing cows," rushed lowing toward the ocean. Indra then became "the lord of what moves and what remains rested." Vritra was the symbol of pre-Aryan power, "warder" of the *"dāsa* lord"; hence the hymn that tells of the battle between Indra and Vritra may be viewed as of historic as well as cosmogonic significance, conveying the essence of the Aryan victory. It has, indeed, been suggested that Vritra was no demon at all, but a dam constructed across the Indus by pre-Aryans to control the river for irrigation agriculture, and that by destroying that "barrier" or "cover" the Aryans flooded the region and its great cities, facilitating their conquest.

Early Gods

Once Indra's victory was achieved, however, Varuna, the King of Universal Order (initially *rita* and later *dharma*) stepped forward to take the central position of Aryan religious authority. Presiding over the sun-filled sky, Varuna was the divine lord of justice "who has spread out the earth, as the butcher does the hide, by way of a carpet for the sun . . . extended the air above the trees . . . put strength in horses, milk in cows, willpower in hearts, fire in waters, the sun in the heaven, and soma upon the mountain." Varuna was the divine judge of Aryan India, and appeals for mercy would be chanted to him by those who strayed from the path of virtue. Older and wiser than Indra, Varuna was most honored by the Aryans, the elder statesman on high, closely connected with the sun god Surya and with one of his lesser manifestations in the Rig Veda, Vishnu, who later shared with Shiva virtual monotheistic dominance over Hinduism.

Agni was god of fire, and as such had many forms, traversing the three realms of earth, atmosphere, and heaven. He was needed for every sacrifice; he mirrored the sun; and he had the power to heal, save, defend, or destroy. Hailed as "offspring of the (primeval) waters," he was also called "illuminator of darkness," and as the many-tongued deity of the sacred altar he presided over "ritual function." Soma was the god of immortality, the nectar whose "glorious drops" impart "freedom" and protect one's body from disease. "May we enjoy with an enlivened spirit the juice thou givest like ancestral riches," chanted the Aryans to divine Soma. "O Soma, King, prolong thou our existence . . . favour us and make us prosper. . . . For thou hast settled in each joint, O Soma."

Among the lesser personified-powers of nature worshipped by the Vedic Aryans, the loveliest was Ushas, the dawn, "rosy-fingered" daughter of the sky. For her most beautiful poems were chanted. She brought of all "lights the fairest."

The Search for Meaning

The seeming simplicity of the Aryan nature-worshipping religion was soon obscured by the Vedic quest for an understanding of cosmic origins and control over cosmic forces. The immediate purpose of a sacrifice was to secure some divine favor, whether fortune, longevity, or progeny, but it also had cosmic meaning in that its proper performance helped maintain the balance of order in the universe. The Aryan householder gave his gods soma, *ghi* (clarified butter), and other delicacies not simply in return for their favors, but because it was his duty to propitiate them so, just as they in turn were obliged to act in the appropriate fashion toward him. For gods as well as men had their individual duties, which were part of the cosmic scheme of things, and only when all behaved properly would the universe function as it was designed to do—in accord with the *rita*, the true order. Demons of falsehood were always trying to destroy that perfect balance, starting floods, bringing drought or famine, appearing in the guise of tigers or mad elephants; they were ever present as mosquitos and other evil creatures that buzzed, crawled, or walked upon the earth. The balance was tenuous at all times, which was why so many sacrifices were required, and why brahmans had to be employed day and night to chant the hymns they memorized. Truth . . . could always be subverted by falsehood . . . just as the "real". . . or existent world might always be disguised by imagined or "unreal". . . illusions, fantasies, and nonexistent fears and terrors. The word *sat*, which originally meant "existent," came thus to be equated with cosmic reality and its underlying ethical principle, truth. To Vedic man the universe was divided between earth's fair surface and the heavenly dome above it, the realm in which *sat* prevailed, and the demon-darkness beneath this world, where unreality and falsehood dominated all. Indra's daily battle renewed the wonder of creation, but speculation about this mighty hero soon led to profound questions: "Who ever saw him? Who is he that we should praise him?"

Before the Rig Veda was finished, such speculation was responsible for the creation of a number of superdeities, whose all-embracing qualities and impersonal characteristics more nearly resembled monotheistic than pantheistic gods. Prajāpati, whose name means "Lord of Creatures," emerged as a more comprehensive god than Indra, as did Visvakarman, the "Maker of All," and Brāhmanāspati, "Lord of the Sacred Utterance (brahman)." The introduction of the last name clearly connotes the growing power and presumption of the brahman priests, who further exalted their ritual chantings by deifying "speech" itself as the goddess Vāc. The evolution of a monistic principle of creation, however, came only at the very end of the Rig Veda (Book X, hymn 129), when we find a neuter pronoun and numeral, Tad Ekam, "That One," cited as the source of all creation, anticipating differentiation of any sort and all deities, self-existent, self-generating, unique. . . .

By about 1000 B.C., then, India's Aryans were asking questions and positing hypothetical solutions to problems that still remain unfathomable. In crediting self-incubating "heat" (*tapas*) with the origin of creation, the Rig Veda sounds so surprisingly scientific that we may find it difficult to reconcile such latter-day sophistication with much of the Rig Veda's earlier naiveté. The word *tapas*, however, was subsequently used in relation to yogic contemplation, and its use in the Rig Veda may reflect the reemergence of India's oldest form of religion as well as "science," the self-imposed rigor of isolated meditation that gave birth to so many illuminating insights throughout Indian history. "Desire" (*kāma*), which later came to mean "love," was the source of That One's stirring to life, the force behind creation, moving even a neuter spirit to sow the first "seed of mind," as it was so often to move India's noblest sages and gods from the austere depths of their contemplation to peaks of passionate bliss. Had pre-Aryan yogis (such as the one depicted on the seal from Mohenjodaro) learned by now the language of their conquerors, teaching their own secrets in turn to brahman bards? Was India's "heat" and ancient wisdom starting already to take its toll of youthful Aryan energy and optimistic self-assurance?

The Hindu Creation Story

from the Rig-Veda

The following selection is from the Rig-Veda, a text generally held to be among the first written in India. The Rig-Veda is thought to have been written down around the year 1000 B.C. in north India, although it may have been preserved as part of oral tradition, passed down through recitation and memorization, for centuries before that. Consisting of over one thousand hymns and prayers meant to be used in sacrificial and other rituals, the Rig-Veda is the most important of the Vedas, the earliest Hindu religious texts. Others include the Sama-Veda, a rearrangement of the hymns in the Rig-Veda; the Atharva-Veda consisting mostly of chants and spells; and the Yajur-Veda, containing descriptions of rituals.

This selection describes how the ancient gods created life on earth by sacrificing and then dismembering Purusha, whom the translator depicts as the original Person. Purusha was the original male principle and his female counterpart was known as Viraj. Among the central features of this dismemberment was the creation of the caste system; its description in the Rig-Veda provides the caste system with an ancient spiritual justification few Hindus question.

Wendy Doniger O'Flaherty, editor and translator, "Rig Veda," *Textual Sources for the Study of Hinduism*. Manchester, UK: Manchester University Press, 1988. Copyright © 1988 by Wendy Doniger O'Flaherty. Reproduced by permission of the publisher.

The Person has a thousand heads, a thousand eyes, a thousand feet. He pervaded the earth on all sides and extended beyond it as far as ten fingers. It is the Person who is all this, whatever has been and whatever is to be. He is the ruler of immortality, when he grows beyond everything through food. Such is his greatness, and the Person is yet more than this. All creatures are a quarter of him; three quarters are what is immortal in heaven. With three quarters the Person rose upwards, and one quarter of him still remains here. From this (quarter on earth) he spread out in all directions, into that which eats and that which does not eat. From him Viraj was born, and from Viraj came the Person. When he was born, he ranged beyond the earth behind and before.

When the gods performed the sacrifice with the Person as the offering, spring was the clarified butter, summer the fuel, autumn the oblation. They anointed the Person, the sacrifice born at the beginning, upon the sacred grass. With him the gods, perfected beings, and sages sacrificed. From that sacrifice in which everything was offered, the melted fat was collected, and he made it into those beasts who live in the air, in the forest, and in villages. From that sacrifice in which everything was offered, the verses and chants were born, the metres were born from it, and from it the formulas were born. Horses were born from it, and those other animals that have two rows of teeth; cows were born from it, and from it goats and sheep were born.

When they divided the Person, into how many parts did they apportion him? What do they call his mouth, his two arms and thighs and feet? His mouth became the Brahmin; his arms were made into the Kshatriya (warrior); his thighs the Vaishyas (the people); and from his feet the Shudras (servants) were born. The moon was born from his mind; from his eye the sun was born. Indra and Agni came from his mouth, and from his vital breath the Wind was born. From his navel the middle realm of space arose; from his head the sky evolved. From his two feet came the earth, and the quarters of the sky from his ear. Thus they set the worlds in order.

There were seven enclosing-sticks for him and thrice seven fuel-sticks, when the gods, performing the sacrifice, bound the Person as the sacrificial beast. With the sacrifice the gods sacrificed to the sacrifice. These were the first dharmas. These very powers reached the dome of the sky where dwell the perfected beings, the ancient gods. (*Rig Veda* 10.90)

The Evolution of the Caste System

by Romila Thapar

For Hindus religious beliefs and customs are insepara-
ble from daily life and from social and family organization. One of the ways in which religious life and
worldly life overlap most clearly is through the caste
system, Hindu India's form of social organization and
hierarchy. In the following selection historian Romila
Thapar examines the origins of this system. Its roots,
she claims, lie in the arrival of Aryan migrants from
southwestern Asia into India sometime in the second
millennium B.C. These lighter-skinned newcomers and,
according to some, conquerors, wanted to differentiate
themselves from the darker-skinned *dasas*, or indigenous inhabitants. They therefore expanded their already existing system of social classes to include the
dasas. These social divisions eventually hardened into
castes. For Hindus caste determined one's job, spouse,
sometimes one's diet and place to live, and one's religious duties. Even today, while they are technically il-
legal in democratic India, caste ideas and habits persist,
and the system has been so pervasive that even non-
Hindu Indians such as Muslims or Christians adhere to
certain caste ideas.

The four basic castes in Hinduism are the Brahmans,

Romila Thapar, "The Impact of Aryan Culture," *A History of India*. Vol. 1. Baltimore, MD: Penguin Books, 1966. Copyright © 1966 by Romila Thapar.
Reproduced by permission of Penguin Books, a division of Penguin Group (UK).

or priests; the Kshatriya, or warriors and rulers; the Vaishya, or productive caste; and the Shudra caste of laborers. In addition there exists a large population of outcastes or untouchables. Beyond this basic structure, as Thapar indicates, is *Jati* or the network of occupational subcastes such as fishermen or cart-drivers. Most Hindus believe that only the highest caste, the Brahmans, is near to *moksha* or release from the wheel of existence. All others can expect to be reborn through many lifetimes of performing such caste duties as the proper marriage and practice of religious rites. Romila Thapar was a professor of history at the University of Delhi in India.

When the Aryans first came to India they were divided into three social classes, the warriors or aristocracy, the priests, and the common people. There was no consciousness of caste, as is clear from remarks such as 'a bard am I, my father is a leech and my mother grinds corn'. Professions were not hereditary, nor were there any rules limiting marriages within these classes, or taboos on whom one could eat with. The three divisions merely facilitated social and economic organization. The first step in the direction of caste (as distinct from class) was taken when the Aryans treated the Dasas as beyond the social pale, probably owing to a fear of the Dasas and the even greater fear that assimilation with them would lead to a loss of Aryan identity. Ostensibly the distinction was largely that of colour, the Dasas being darker and of an alien culture. The Sanskrit word for caste, *varna*, actually means colour. The colour element of caste was emphasized, throughout this period, and was eventually to become deep-rooted in north-Indian Aryan culture. Initially, therefore, the division was between the Aryans and the non-Aryans. The Aryans were the *dvija* or twice-born castes (the first being physical birth and the second the initiation into caste status), consisting of the *kshatriyas* (warriors and aristocracy), the *brahmans* (priests), and the *vaishyas* (cultivators); the fourth caste, the *shudras*, were the Dasas and those of mixed Aryan-Dasa origin.

Caste Flexibility

The actual mechanism of caste was not a formal division of society into four broad groups. The first three castes were probably a theoretical framework evolved by the brahmans, into which they systematically arranged various professions. Combinations and permutations within the latter were inevitable and were explained as originating in the inter-mixing of castes. The fourth caste, however, appears to have been based both on race as well as occupation (as was also the case later with the emergency of the out-castes, whose position was so low that in later centuries even their touch was held to be polluting). The caste status of an occupation could change over a long period. Gradually the Aryan *vaishyas* became traders and landowners and the *shudras* moved up the scale to become the cultivators (though not in the condition of serfs). Aryan ascendancy over the Dasas was now complete. But although the *shudras* were permitted to cultivate the land, they were still excluded from *dvija* status, and were to remain so, an exclusion which prevented them from participating in Vedic ritual and led them to worship their own gods. This vertical division of society made it easier in later centuries to accept new ethnic groups. Each new group to arrive in India took on the characteristics of a separate sub-caste and was thereby assimilated into the larger caste structure. The position of the new sub-caste in the hierarchy was dependent on its occupation and, on occasion, on its social origins.

The establishment of caste was no doubt promoted by other factors as well, and the process by which the *shudras* became cultivators is inherent in these factors. With the transition from nomadic pastoralism to a settled agrarian economy, specialization of labour gradually became a marked feature of Aryan society. The clearing of the forests and the existence of new settlements led to the emergence of a trading community engaged in the supply and exchange of goods. There was thus a natural separation between the agriculturists, those who cleared and colonized the land, and the traders, those who established the economic links between the settlements, the latter coming from the class of wealthier landowners who could afford economic speculation. The priests were in any case a group by themselves. The warriors, led by the king, believed their function to be solely that of protection, on which function the entire well-being of each community depended. The king emerged as the dominant power, and the warriors (*kshatriyas*) were therefore of the first rank in caste. The priests (brahmans) came next, followed by the more prosperous landowners and traders (*vaishyas*), and finally the cultivators (*shudras*).

Caste and Religion

The priests were not slow to realize the significance of such a division of society and the supreme authority which could be invested in the highest caste. They not only managed to usurp the first position by claiming that they alone could bestow divinity on the king (which was by now essential to kingship) but they also gave religious sanction to caste divisions. A late hymn of the *Rig-Veda* provides a mythical origin of the castes:

> When the gods made a sacrifice with the Man
>   as their victim. . . .
> When they divided the Man, into how many
>   parts did they divide him?
> What was his mouth, what were his arms,
>   what were his thighs and his feet called?
> The brahman was his mouth, of his arms were
>   made the warrior.
> His thighs became the vaishya, of his feet the
>   shudra was born.
> With Sacrifice the gods sacrificed to Sacrifice,
>   these were the first of the sacred laws.
> These mighty beings reached the sky, where
>   are the eternal spirits, the gods.

The continuance of caste was secured by its being made hereditary: the primitive taboo on commensality (eating together) became a caste law, and this in turn made it necessary to define marriage limits, leading to elaborate rules of endogamy and exogamy. The basis and continuance of the caste system depended not on the four-fold division but on the vast network of sub-castes, which was intimately connected with occupation. Eventually, the sub-caste (*jati*, literally 'birth') came to have more relevance for the day-to-day working of Hindu society than the main caste (*varna*), since the functioning of society was dependent on sub-caste relationships and adjustments, the *varna* remaining an over-all theoretical framework. Sub-caste relationships were based on specialization of work and economic interdependence. With caste becoming hereditary, and the close connexion between occupation and sub-caste, there was an automatic check on individuals moving up in the hierarchy of castes. Vertical mobility was possible to the sub-caste as a whole and depended upon the entire group acting as one and changing both its location and its work. An individual could express his protest only by joining a sect which disavowed caste, such as were to evolve from the sixth century B.C. onwards.

Basic Hindu Beliefs

by David M. Knipe

Hinduism is extremely complex, and in comparison to the other great world religions, it can be difficult to grasp. Hinduism has no founder, for instance, comparable to the original Buddha or to Jesus of Nazareth. Nor does it have a single basic text or common body of rituals or practices. Nevertheless, as David M. Knipe points out in the following selection, virtually all Hindus share a few basic beliefs, and these beliefs evolved over a very long period of time. He suggests that these are summed up in the Laws of Manu, a collection of ethical texts compiled sometime between 200 B.C. and A.D. 200.

For Hindus the overarching goal is for their souls to achieve *moksha*, or release from the wheel of existence. In order for this to happen the soul must be reborn, or reincarnated, into new bodies over thousands of lifetimes. During any given individual lifetime, however, people are expected to fulfill certain duties which depend on their caste and gender. If they fail to fulfill those duties, which are broadly known as dharma, or if they commit evil acts, they run the risk of piling up bad karma, meaning their souls will be reborn farther away from rather than closer to *moksha*. Members of the highest, priestly, caste, the Brahmans, tend to have the most duties, as Knipe indicates. While two other castes, the warrior Kshatriya and the productive Vaishya, are, like the Brahmans, "twiceborn," the lowest caste, the laboring Shudra, believe they are the farthest away from release from the wheel of birth and death.

Beyond these beliefs, that Knipe suggests are even over the last centuries being modified by changing conditions, Hinduism remains multifaceted, a religion of many gods, practices, sects, and rituals. David M. Knipe is the chair of the Department of South Asian Studies and the Religious Studies Program at the University of Wisconsin–Madison.

———————

Hinduism can be seen to develop over a period of more than three thousand years, with significant contributions entering the tradition continuously. Such a breadth of historical experience in addition multicultural and regional diversity might excuse the Hindu tradition from any concise or simple definition. Nevertheless, a pattern of beliefs and practices emerged over time on which both ancient and modern Hindus might agree.

One concise statement appeared about the beginning of the Common Era in what came to be an authoritative text of classical Hindu law, the Laws of Manu, or Manava Dharma Shastra. Traditionally this Sanskrit text was compiled by the sage Manu as one of several digests concerned with religion, law, right conduct—all that is encompassed in the Sanskrit word *dharma*. Manu declared that a person may concentrate on liberation from the world of continuous rebirths only after paying off three debts. Manu's statement is a good working definition of Hinduism because it focuses upon the central concerns of the ongoing tradition.

The flow of existence is known in classical Hinduism

as transmigration (*samsara*), a dilemma to be solved by release (*moksha*) from bondage to this world brought about by the consequences of action (*karma*). Manava Dharma Shastra 6.35 reflects the historical development of Hinduism, as well as its powerful conservatism. Manu's phrase combines the individual's three debts, a belief that was already a thousand years old in Manu's day, with the notion that an individual experiences continuous cycles of births and deaths in this world, a more recent doctrine.

A Hindu's Three Debts

Turning first to the older belief, the three debts—to the ancient sages, the gods, and the ancestors—are first described about 1000 BCE in sacred texts known as the Vedas. Three obligations are said to be incurred at birth by everyone in the elite class of priests and scholars known as Brahmans, and they should be paid to the mythical sages who first transmitted the Vedas, to the gods, and to the ancestors or collective "Fathers" as they are known. A Brahman becomes free of this natal [birth] liability by learning and reciting the eternal Vedas (thereby passing on as the ancient sages did in the beginning), by sacrificing to the gods (thereby continuing the world that was created by sacrifice in the beginning), and by producing a son (thereby continuing a lineage as the Fathers did in the beginning). Freedom from such debts was a spiritual fulfillment, as emancipation from the routine of a householder reciting the three sacred texts and tending his three sacred fires.

By the time the Laws of Manu were compiled, however, several significant transitions had occurred to provide a new context for this belief in three basic obligations. For one, the notion of three debts at birth applied to all three "twiceborn" classes—the Brahmans, the warriors, and the producers. In other words, the whole of the three-level society was involved as a unit distinguished from an alien world outside the authority of these sacred texts and rituals. Second, the worldview in Manu's time was radically altered from the one that had prevailed in 1000 BCE. Attention now focused upon release from bondage to this painful world of *samsara*, upon an adequate means of dealing with the consequences of action, *karma*, a cosmic impersonal accounting that causes rebirth. And third, the Laws of Manu suggest in this same passage that a Brahman householder may transcend domestic life by incorporating his three sacred fires within himself in order to take up the renunciant ascetic [one who forsakes possessions and human relationships] path in the forest.

Thus all the ingredients by which classical Hinduism is defined are present in this Laws of Manu segment. *Samsara* and *karma* are basic facts of the human condition, and *moksha* the ultimate aim of the spiritual life. The path toward liberation from the round of births and deaths involves recognition of the eternal Vedas and the ancient sages . . . who made them available, worship of the gods . . . who created this universe, and responsible regard for the Fathers . . . with continuation of their lineage into the future. But the path also involves an idealized fourfold program for life that proceeds from study of the sacred texts—the student . . . absorbs sacred knowledge—to the life of the married householder (within children, civic responsibilities, and sacred tasks such as worship of the family deities), to the chaste simplicity of the forest-dwelling stage and intensification of the spiritual quest. The fourth and final stage is that of the *samnyasin*, the renunciant who interiorizes his sacred fires and is detached from actions that bind.

Stages of Life

Matching this fourfold program of life stages, known as *ashramas*, is a set of four goals of life for every Hindu, also sequential: the pursuits of sexual love (*kama*), wealth or material gain (*artha*), spiritual conduct or duty (*dharma*), and liberation (*moksha*). *Moksha* transcends the preceding three pursuits as the *samnyasin* transcends his previous three life stages.

In the two millennia that separate such classical texts as Manu's from the Hinduism of regional South Asia today a great deal has transpired. Attention shifted from the great body of texts known as Vedas to equally huge collections of epic recitations and performances, as well as other new genres of oral mythology and tradition. The focus on sacrifice in the Vedic mode gradually gave way to worship of and devotional expression to a powerful set of deities including the older gods Vishnu and Shiva and newer goddesses such as Durga or Kali. The structure of society became increasingly complicated as the class hierarchy gave way to a regionally varied and more intensely stratified caste system. And along the way Hinduism was frequently threatened and then benefited by encounters with other faith traditions, including Jainism and Buddhism, and subsequently Christianity, Zoroastrianism, and Islam.

In sum, if we were to identify a Hindu in India, Nepal, or elsewhere in South Asia today, he or she would no doubt believe in *karma* and *samsara*, revere certain texts and certain deities (usually without naming a single text or deity as requisite), accept the obligation of satisfying his or her older ancestors with progeny and with more or less regular offerings and prayers, declare class and caste status within a social structure that most of Hindus would recognize, demonstrate certain ascetic tendencies in the form of fasts and vows, and describe certain progress or intentions in life goals and pursuits toward an ultimate release (although for many the ideal of *moksha* is a remote target of the far end of an inevitable series of rebirths).

Continuity and Change

In other words the broad definition of Hinduism today is very nearly what it was more than two millennia ago in the classical period. Two important changes might be registered here, however. One is the deepening base of Hinduism in the folk and tribal traditions of every region of the subcontinent. Those who were "alien" in the period of the early Vedas and "excluded" in the time of Manu have in many respects come to be the dominant forces in the currents of Hinduism over the millennia, and their traditions are now mingled irreversibly into the mainstream. The other change is to the gender base. We noted that the debt to the Fathers is paid by producing a son (not just a child) according to this male-dominated tradition, and everywhere in Vedic, classical, medieval, and modern Hinduism the paradigms in myths, rituals, doctrines, and symbols are masculine. But just as goddesses traditions encroached successfully on the territory of masculine deities, so too has the impact of women's religious activity, the ritual life in particular, been of increasing significance in the overall scale of Hindu tradition. To put this another way, in traditional life the unlettered folk have always shaped Hinduism, and half of them have been women. It is not feminine roles in Hinduism that have been lacking but rather the acknowledgment of such in literature, the arts, and institutions such as the priesthood and temple and monastic administrations. Only now, in a world rapidly changing because of educational opportunities, are such institutions and media beginning to reflect accurately the total picture of Hindu class, caste, gender, and regional life.

High-Caste Marriage According to the Laws of Manu

from the Laws of Manu

The following selection is from the Laws of Manu, one of the most important Hindu texts. Unlike the ancient Vedas, texts consisting mostly of chants, prayers, and rituals, or the epic poems the *Mahabharata* or the *Ramayana*, the Laws of Manu is concerned mostly with how Hindus should conduct their daily lives and how everyday life is connected with spiritual life and the larger universe. Scholars believe that it was written sometime in the first or second century A.D., and it is purported to be the work of the sage Manu, who is likely a mythical figure. It is often referred to, as is the Christian Bible, using chapter and verse numbers.

The selection is concerned with proper marriage for twice-born, or higher-caste, Hindus. The text makes clear those women who are desirable for such men and those who should be avoided. Proper marriages conducted according to the proper rituals, the author or authors assert, will result not only in satisfaction and happiness for both husband and wife, but in devoted, accomplished, long-lived children. The text also notes that the gods are happiest and the family is strongest when wife and mother are respected and revered.

Wendy Doniger and Brian K. Smith, translators, "Chapter 3," *The Laws of Manu*. New York: Penguin Books, 1991. Copyright © 1991 by Wendy Doniger and Brian K. Smith. Reproduced by permission of the publisher.

When he has received his guru's permission and bathed and performed the ritual for homecoming according to the rules, a twice-born man should marry a wife who is of the same class and has the right marks.[1] A woman who is neither a co-feeding relative on her mother's side nor belongs to the same lineage (of the sages) on her father's side, and who is a virgin, is recommended for marriage to twice-born men. When a man connects himself with a woman, he should avoid the ten following families, even if they are great, or rich in cows, goats, sheep, property, or grain: a family that has abandoned the rites, or does not have male children, or does not chant the Veda; and those families in which they have hairy bodies, piles, consumption, weak digestion, epilepsy, white leprosy, or black leprosy.

A man should not marry a girl who is a redhead or has an extra limb or is sickly or has no body hair or too much body hair or talks too much or is sallow; or who is named after a constellation, a tree, or a river, or who has a low-caste name, or is named after a mountain, a bird, a snake, or has a menial or frightening name. He should marry a woman who does not lack any part of her body and who has a pleasant name, who walks like a goose or an elephant,[2] whose body hair and hair on the head is fine, whose teeth are not big, and who has delicate limbs. A wise man will not marry a woman who has no brother or whose father is unknown, for fear that she may be an appointed daughter or that he may act wrongly.

1. In Vedic times, and to some extent in present-day India among certain priests, men traced their descent through a ritual lineage (*gotra*) to one of the seven mythical sages or *ṛṣis* (*rishis*) to whom the Veda was first revealed.   2. The goose (*haṃsa*) and elephant (*vāraṇa*) walk with a rolling gait that ancient Indian poets considered a sign of beauty in a woman.

A woman of the same class is recommended to twice-born men for the first marriage; but for men who are driven by desire, these are the women, in progressively descending order: According to tradition, only a servant woman can be the wife of a servant; she and one of his own class can be the wife of a commoner; these two and one of his own class for a king; and these three and one of his own class for a priest. Not a single story mentions a servant woman as the wife of a priest or a ruler, even in extremity. Twice-born men who are so infatuated as to marry women of low caste quickly reduce their families, including the descendants, to the status of servants. A man falls when he weds a servant woman, according to Atri and to (Gautama) the son of Utathya, or when he has a son by her, according to Śaunaka, or when he has any children by her, according to Bhṛgu [Atri, Gautama, Utathya, Śaunaka, and Bhṛgu are Hindu sages]. A priest who climbs into bed with a servant woman goes to hell; if he begets a son in her, he loses the status of priest. The ancestors and the gods do not eat the offerings to the gods, to the ancestors, and to guests that such a man makes with her, and so he does not go to heaven. No redemption is prescribed for a man who drinks the saliva from the lips of a servant woman or is tainted by her breath or begets a son in her. . . .

Arranged Marriages Are Best

It is said to be the law of Brahmā when a man dresses his daughter and adorns her and he himself gives her as a gift to a man he has summoned, one who knows the revealed canon and is of good character. They call it the law of the gods when a man adorns his daughter and, in the course of a sacrifice, gives her as a gift to the officiating priest who is properly performing the ritual. It is called the sages' law when he gives away his daughter by the rules, after receiving from the bridegroom a cow and a bull, or two cows and bulls, in accordance with the law. The tradition calls it the rule of the Lord of Creatures when a man gives away his daughter after adorning her and saying 'May the two of you together fulfil your duties.'

It is called the demonic law when a man takes the girl because he wants her himself, when he has given as much wealth as he can to her relatives and to the girl herself. It is to be recognized as a centaur marriage when the girl and her lover join with one another in sexual union because they want to, out of desire. It is called the rule of the ogres when a man forcibly carries off a girl out of her house, screaming and weeping, after he has killed, wounded, and broken. The lowest and most evil of marriages, known as that of the ghouls, takes place when a man secretly has sex with a girl who is asleep, drunk, or out of her mind. For priests, the gift of a girl with (a libation of) water is the best (marriage); but for the other classes (the best is) when they desire one another.

The Results of a Good Marriage

Listen, priests, while I tell you fully about all the qualities of these marriages that Manu has proclaimed. If a son born to a woman who has had a Brahmā marriage does good deeds, he frees from guilt ten of the ancestors who came before him, ten later descendants, and himself as the twenty-first. A son born to a woman who had a marriage of the gods (frees) seven ancestors and seven descendants, a son born to a woman who had a marriage of the sages (frees) three (of each), and a son born to a woman who had a marriage of the Lord of Creatures (frees) six (of each). The sons born from these four marriages, in order beginning with the Brahmā marriage, are filled with the splendour of the Veda and are esteemed by educated men. Beautiful and endowed with the quality of lucidity, rich and famous, enjoying life to the fullest, most religious, they live for a hundred years. But from those (four) other remaining bad marriages are born cruel sons, liars who hate the Veda and religion. Out of blameless marriages with women come blameless progeny. Blameworthy progeny come to men from blameworthy (marriages); therefore one should avoid the blameworthy ones.

The transformative ritual of taking the bride by the hand is prescribed for women of the same class; know that this (following) procedure is for the marriage ritual with women of a different class. When a woman marries a man of superior class, a woman of the ruler class must take hold of an arrow, a commoner girl a whip, and a servant woman must grasp the fringe of (his) garment.

A man should have sex with his wife during her fertile season, and always find his satisfaction in his own wife; when he desires sexual pleasure he should go to her to whom he is vowed, except on the days at the (lunar) junctures. The natural fertile season of women is traditionally said to last for sixteen nights, though these include four special days that good people despise. Among these (nights), the first four, the eleventh, and the thirteenth are disapproved; the other ten nights are approved. On the even nights, sons are conceived, and on the uneven nights, daughters; therefore a man who wants sons should unite with his wife during her fertile season on the even nights. A male child is born when the semen of the man is greater (than that of the woman), and a female child when (the semen) of the woman is greater (than that of the man); if both are equal, a hermaphrodite is born, or a boy and a girl; and if (the semen) is weak or scanty, the opposite will occur.[3] A man who avoids women on the (six) disapproved nights and on eight other nights is regarded as chaste, no matter which of the four stages of life he is in.

No learned father should take a bride-price for his daughter, no matter how small, for a man who, out of greed, exacts a bride-price would be selling his child like a pimp.

And those deluded relatives who live off a woman's property—her carriages, her clothes, and so on—are evil and go to hell. Some say that the cow and bull (given) during the (wedding) of the sages is a bride-price, but it is not so. No matter how great or small (the price), the sale amounts to prostitution. Girls whose relatives do not take the bride-price for themselves are not prostituted; that (gift) is merely honorific and a mercy to maidens.

Wives Are to Be Revered and Adorned

Fathers, brothers, husbands, and brothers-in-law who wish for great good fortune should revere these women and adorn them. The deities delight in places where women are revered, but where women are not revered all rites are fruitless. Where the women of the family are miserable, the family is soon destroyed, but it always thrives where the women are not miserable. Homes that are cursed by women of the family who have not been

3. The final instance would be a child with no sexual organs at all, or a miscarriage, or no conception at all.

treated with due reverence are completely destroyed, as if struck down by witchcraft. Therefore men who wish to prosper should always revere these women with ornaments, clothes, and food at celebrations and festivals.

There is unwavering good fortune in a family where the husband is always satisfied by the wife, and the wife by the husband. If the wife is not radiant she does not stimulate the man; and because the man is unstimulated the making of children does not happen. If the woman is radiant, the whole family is radiant, but if she is not radiant the whole family is not radiant. Through bad marriages, the neglect of rites, failure to study the Veda, and transgressing against priests, families cease to be families.

CHAPTER 2

The Expansion of Hinduism

Brahma, Shiva, and Vishnu: The Main Hindu Gods

by David S. Noss and John B. Noss

Hinduism is a polytheistic religion. According to folklore, these gods number in the hundreds of millions. By the time that Hinduism matured in the first millennium A.D., however, most Hindus worshipped one of three gods: Brahma, Shiva, or Vishnu. Or, alternatively, they worshipped one of the avatars of Shiva or Vishnu. Avatars are gods in another form or another incarnation. In the case of Shiva, arguably the most popular of the Hindu gods, his avatars include his various female consorts, such as Kali, Parvati, or Durga, or his son, the elephant-headed Ganesha. Hindus believe that by worshipping one of these avatars, one ultimately worships Shiva as well. Vishnu, for his part, is generally worshipped as one of nine known avatars, a list that includes Siddhartha Gautama, the founder of Buddhism. Likewise, the worship of one of these avatars always goes back to Vishnu.

In the following selection, religious scholars David S. Noss and John B. Noss examine the natures of Hinduism's most prominent gods as well as their appearances in ritual, literature, and folklore. They pay particular attention to Rama and Krishna, two of Vishnu's avatars, who play starring roles in, respectively, the *Ra-*

mayana and the *Mahabharata*, the great Hindu epics. Implicit throughout is the notion that in Hinduism all gods are merely aspects of the divine, that ultimately, as Hindus claim "god is one, but it is known by many names." David S. Noss is professor of religion at Heidelberg College. The late John B. Noss was professor of religion at Franklin and Marshall College and author of *Man's Religions*, a commonly used textbook for four decades.

Of the three great gods, Brahmā, the Creator, is the least widely worshiped. . . . Scarcely half a dozen temples are now dedicated to him. He may be compared with the "high god of primitive peoples," no longer active on earth after having finished the work of creation. Yet he is deeply respected. In art he is depicted as a kingly personage with four heads, severely reading the Vedas, and is shown riding a white wild goose, symbolic of his aloofness.

Shiva: The Creator and Destroyer

Shiva is one of the great gods of Asia. His followers have given him the title Mahadeva, "the great god," and he measures up to the name. His character is most complex and has some fascinating aspects. As the later form of the dread god Rudra of Vedic days, he still is (in an important aspect) the Destroyer. In the words of the *Yajur-Veda*, he is "the threatener, the slayer, the vexer, and the afflicter." His presence is felt "in the fall of the leaf," and he is the bringer of disease and death, and, hence, a "man-slayer." His presence is felt at the funeral pyre, and he should be honored there. But he is not purely evil. His name shows that he is, or can be made, "auspicious" (shiva). It is of some interest to speculate about the origin of this name. At the end of the Vedic Age Rudra seems to have been so feared that his name was never mentioned. This was all in the spirit of the European proverb, "Speak of the devil, and he is sure to appear." Like the peasants of Europe in similar circumstances, the Indo-Aryans spoke of him preferably through descriptive titles. At length the word *shiva*, at first applied to other deities also, came to stand for him alone. Not only *could* he be auspicious, if he would, but perhaps a flattering reference to him as such would *make* him so?

Moreover, there were reasons for believing he had a constructive and helpful aspect. Originally, he was a mountain-god given to destructive and punitive raids on the plains, but those who penetrated to his mountain fastnesses discovered that under his kindly care grew medicinal herbs for the healing of men and women. Could it be that his sole interest was destruction? Was not his coming often "a blessing in disguise"? Gradually it came to be felt that Shiva destroyed in order to make room for new creation. . . .

After all, pure destructiveness achieves no lasting results in tropical countries; the death and decay of vegetation is but the prelude to the rise of new forms of life, all the more vigorous for having humus to feed on. Besides, in a land where reincarnation is an accepted belief, death means almost instantaneous release into new life. By suggestions flowing from realizations such as this, the functions of Shiva received a meaningful enlargement.

He became identified with the processes of reproduction in every realm of life—vegetable, animal, and human. He seemed to have taken over the phallic emblems and characteristics of the fertility-gods of pre-Aryan India. The sex-energy that was identified with him was represented to the eyes of his worshipers by the *lingam* and *yoni*, conventional emblems of the male and female reproductive organs. With a reverent sense of the mystery of divine and human creative force, Shiva's worshipers, in their homes as well as in their temples, approach these symbols in devout worship. In the same reverent spirit the Shiva-worshiping sect founded in the twelfth century C.E., called the Lingayats, numbering some three millions today, carry with them, usually in a capsule hung around the neck, a soapstone lingam without which they would never think of appearing in public.

The Dance of Birth and Death

By a further development of this association of ideas, Shiva stands for Life itself, as pure energy or force. He is often shown dancing on the squirming body of the demon of delusion, with his four arms gracefully waving in the air, one hand holding a small drum, another a flame or fire-pot. Poised on one leg, his whole figure shows a tremendous vitality, and it is felt that the dance is speeding the cycles of birth and death. Further evidences of vitality are suggested by endowing Shiva with a third eye placed vertically in the middle of the forehead and picturing him as having a blue body and a dark throat encircled by a necklace of serpents. Some of his images display him with five or six faces varying in expression, all of which, taken together, suggest his multiple attributes and energies.

At first view it may come as a surprise that Shiva is also the patron of ascetics and holy men. He is often represented as being himself deep in meditation, his naked body smeared with ashes and his hair braided after the fashion of an ascetic. The rationale of the ascription to him of ascetic interests seems to be something like this: the ascetic "destroys" his lower self to allow his higher or spiritual self to come to expression; the body must be curbed to free the soul; all worldly affections and lusts must be rooted out. The result will be a great access of power. But such regeneration is just what Shiva most desires to further. He is therefore on the side of the ascetics. . . .

Shiva's Consorts and Associates

That Shiva has come to represent life-energy in all its aspects is amply attested by the character of his various consorts and associates. His divine spouse or Devi is many persons in one and bears different names in the various regions of India. As Parvati, "the mountaineer," or Uma, "light," she is gracious and kind. As Durga, "the unapproachable," Chandi, "the wild," or Kali, "the black," she is helpful and baleful and the terrible at once; a spreader of disease, thereby awaking men's terror, yet an implacable enemy of the demons, thereby filling them with gratitude; kindly to her favored ones, yet accustomed to devour humans and animals. Durga, the unapproachable, has been the patroness of the robber caste bearing the name of Thugs. Kali, the black, wears around her dark neck a necklace of skulls and uses her four strong arms as flails to demolish her victims before she fills her mouth with their flesh, but she is infinitely generous and kind to those whom she loves and who love her in return. In Bengal she is adored as the great Mother; mystics and seers like Ramakrishna and Vivekananda have devoted themselves to her with the most intense kind of passionate attachment (bhakti).

Associated with Shiva also are Ganesha, the elephant-headed god, and Nandi, the white bull. Ganesha is Shiva's son by Parvati, his mountaineer consort. The elephant head, found everywhere in Shiva's temples, symbolizes Ganesha's cunning and his elephantlike ability to remove obstacles by great strength. Nandi, whose milk-white or black bull-image reclines in Shiva's temples, and whose representative, the live white bull, wanders in the temple courts and down the streets in freedom, is Shiva's temple chamberlain and the guardian of quadrupeds. . . .

Vishnu: The Preserver

The third member of the great Hindu triad is called the Preserver. He is always benevolent, primarily the conservator of values and an active agent in their realization. Unlike the complex Shiva, he is the perfect and patient exemplar of winsome divine Love. He watches from the skies, and whenever he sees values threatened or the good in peril, he exerts all his preservative influence in their behalf. He therefore rivals Shiva in popularity among the masses. The stories of his divine activity attract a growing following. He is usually represented with four arms, in two hands holding the symbols of his royal power, the mace and the discus, and in two others the emblems of his magic power and stainless purity, the conch and the lotus respectively. His head is surmounted by a high crown and diadem, his feet are blue, his vesture yellow, and he has the lotus eyes so much admired by Hindus. When reclining, he is shown resting on the world-serpent, Shesha or Ananta; his vehicle is the bird Garuda, and a fish is his symbol. His shakti or spouse is the lovely goddess of fortune and beauty, Lakshmi.

Vishnu's rise to high popular favor is in part due to Vedic mythology. In the Vedas, as we have seen, he is a solar deity. Taking their cue from the fact that the sun redeems the earth from darkness in his passage between earth and sky, the Vedic people developed the myth relating how, when the demon-king Bali seized control of the earth, Vishnu appeared in the form of a dwarf and meekly asked and obtained from the amused giant the promise of as much ground as he could traverse in three steps. The bargain concluded, Vishnu at once returned to his own shape and restored heaven and earth to gods and men by encompassing them in two swift strides. By not taking a third stride across hell, he left it in the demon's possession. This myth provided the intimation concerning the character of Vishnu's interests and activity that has led to his rise in popular esteem. It was seen that he "comes to earth" in *avataras* or "descents" when needed. He has not come down once only, his devotees have urged. Besides descending as a dwarf, he was incarnate in Rama, the ideal king of the *Ramayana*, and in Krishna, the warrior-hero and pastoral-lover of the *Mahabharata* and folklore. Indeed, a fast-developing mythology went on to relate that he had had animal as well as human avatars.

Vishnu's Many Forms

The avatars of Vishnu have been traditionally set at ten, though popular belief has much enlarged the number. Of the traditional list, nine avatars are said to have already occurred, while the tenth is yet to come. We have already mentioned three of them. In the other avatars Vishnu became in turn a fish, which rescued the first man, Manu, from being swept away in a world-flood; a tortoise, which swam under Mt. Mandara and assisted the gods in using it to churn the nectar of immortality and other valuable products from the ocean of milk; a boar, which, with its tusks, lifted the sunken earth above the depths of the sea into which it had been plunged; a man-lion, who tore to pieces a demon-father attempting to kill his son because he prayed to Vishnu; a Brahmin warrior-hero, who twenty-one times utterly defeated the Kshatriya caste and finally established Brahmin supremacy; and Gautama, the founder of Buddhism. The tenth avatar is to be that of Kalki, a messiah with a sword of flame, riding on a white horse, who shall come to save the righteous and destroy the wicked at the end of the fourth and depraved world period. (To some the horse is so prominent that they name this avatar the Ashvatara, "the Horse Avatar.")

It is significant that the Buddha is in the list. One suspects the name of the great founder of Buddhism was added to Vishnu's avatars as a tactical maneuver, designed, and successfully too, to reconcile Buddhism and Hinduism. . . .

Vishnu's Most Popular Forms

Incomparably the most popular of the avatars are those of Rama and Krishna. Rama is the ideal man of the Hindu epics, and his wife is the ideal woman. As the *Ramayana* relates, Rama's happy marriage to Sita, a beauteous princess of the royal house of Mithila, was followed by great trouble. The demon-king of Ceylon, Ravana, treacherously seized Sita and carried her off to his island home. In great distress, Rama enlisted the aid of Hanuman, the monkey-general (the earliest detective in world literature, by the way, and now a Hindu god in his own right). The monkey-general was able to conduct an extensive search from the vantage point of the treetops, and Sita was finally found. Rama fought and slew Ravana, and Sita, after successfully passing through an ordeal of fire to prove her chastity, rejoined her mate. Because of the currency in all parts of India of the various versions of the Ramayana, Rama is widely revered. Millions make him the object of their devotion, and his image is often worshiped in a manner to suggest that he is no mere savior-hero but the all-God. There are, in fact, two phases of Rama-worship: (1) reverential respect for Rama as a hero who was an avatar of Vishnu, and (2) theistic worship of Rama, which gives him exclusive devotion as the supreme deity.

It would be interesting to explore, as we cannot here, the theological doctrines evolved as a result of the theistic attitude to Rama. Yet one doctrinal issue calls for mention. It has to do with the famous controversy as to whether Rama saves by the "monkey-hold" or by the "cat-hold"—that is, with an individual's cooperation or without it. One group of Rama devotees contends that Rama saves only through the free cooperation of the believer with him; the believer must cling to the god as a baby monkey clings to its mother when the latter is swinging off to safety through the trees. The other group believes that salvation is of God only, and that Rama saves his chosen ones by carrying them off as a cat carries a kitten by the scruff of the neck.

Krishna and Divine Love

Highly regarded though Rama is, Krishna is even more popular, both as an avatar and as a god. His character is more complex than Rama's, presenting two distinct aspects not a little difficult to reconcile. The *Mahabharata* shows him in one phase, pastoral poetry and folklore in another. In the *Mahabharata* he is serious and severe, a resourceful war-hero. Throughout the strenuous episodes of the epic he seems primarily anxious to direct the attention of all humanity to Vishnu, the god-form of the Absolute, of whom he is the incarnation. In this connection . . . he asks for the unconditioned devotion of true bhakti toward himself as the earthly form of Vishnu, the supreme Lord of the World. The other Krishna is a mischievous and amorous wonder-worker, the pivotal figure in a vast folklore. Hindu imagination has dwelt lovingly on his childhood as a pantry-haunting "butter-thief" and fat little playfellow. Thousands of Hindu women daily worship him in this phase, gazing upon his chubby infant-images with as much devotion as Italian women regard their beloved Bambino, the child Jesus. But this Krishna is more representatively portrayed as an enchanting pastoral figure. In most of the folktales he is a sprightly and amorous cowherd, a melodious flute at his lips, piping as he moves among the cattle the ravishing airs that win him the love of the *gopis* or milkmaids, with whom he dallies in dark-eyed passion. He unites himself with hundreds of these adoring ones, (one Purana says sixteen thousand adoring ones!) but values above all the beautiful Radha, his favorite mistress. The erotic literature that has sprung up to describe this phase of the god's activity bears some resemblance in general tone to the literature of Shaktism [devotion to the "female" aspects of divine energy] though it prefers expression in story to the latter's philosophy and Tantrism.

The sects that give Krishna a more or less exclusive devotion (bhakti) rank him as high as the Rama-worshipers do their paragon. In Bengal one sect sets Radha beside Krishna as his eternal consort and directs worshipers to seek the favor of both diligently, in the hope of being transported at death to the pleasure groves of the Brindaban heaven, where Krishna and Radha make love forever, in ever-young delight. It is not unexpected that the extremes of left-hand Shaktism occur in some Krishna cults, yet virtually all the devotees of Krishna stress love of the god as a spiritual rather than a carnal passion. The infatuation of the gopis for the divinely adorable cowherd is given a symbolic meaning; even their transports of love, the thrilling sensation at the roots of the hair, the choking emotion, and the swooning, are said to give a true picture in sensuous imagery of the exaltation produced in the worshiper who is looking upon the image of Krishna and thinking of his love.

Popular Gods and Goddesses

by Hinduwebsite.com

The following selection comes from a Web site devoted to numerous aspects of Hinduism and life in India. The Web site is maintained by a devotee of Shaivism, or a worshipper of Shiva. Like all devout Hindus, however, the author understands that there are many ways of reaching the divine, and he presents some of these other ways by describing the worship of such popular gods and goddesses as Saraswathi, the goddess of knowledge; Parvati, who is also known as Kali the destroyer; and Ganesha, who is the god responsible for removing obstacles and who is depicted in artwork as having the head of an elephant. As the author notes, all of these gods are known by different names depending, often, on the aspects they take or on the particular part of life or religion they are thought to emphasize during a specific ritual or situation.

Throughout this article the author reminds the reader that, despite the multiplicity of gods and the numerous forms they can take, there is fundamentally only one universal godhead. This godhead is an unknowable eternal force which, where necessary or desirable, incarnates itself as a lesser god, or even sometimes as a human, to provide some sort of service to humanity in the maintenance of cosmic order. These

Hinduwebsite.com, "The Hindu Pantheon FAQ," www.hinduwebsite.com. Reproduced by permission.

incarnations are the gods that most Hindus worship in their regular rituals and, by worshipping them, also worship the one universal godhead.

Why Hindus Worship Many Gods and Goddesses

According to the tenets of Hinduism, the whole universe is pervaded by one Universal God, who is imperishable, indestructible, infinite, without form and beyond human thought. There goes neither the mind, nor the intellect nor the senses and none can truly define Him and comprehend Him. In His unmanifest state He is unknown, vast emptiness or nothingness, and since He is prior to all, no one is actually aware how He wakes up and manifests all this that we know as His creation.

For some unknown, mysterious and inexplicable reasons, He wakes Himself up, setting in process a massive chain reaction that explodes into this gigantic, dynamic, astounding and material universe, which we perceive through our senses and intellect to be this universe. Thus He who is One, beyond and transcendental, descends into the lower levels of His own creation to become many individual things, both living and nonliving, suffused with His tremendous energy, dormant in some, active in some other, and in varying degrees of purity and permanence evolution and involution.

Of this diversity so produced, some are divinities, some are ordinary beings, some demons and evil beings and some purely inconscient and inert. The divinities, whom we recognize in Hinduism as gods and goddesses, possess tremendous energies, higher knowledge and unified wisdom and inhabit the higher planes or worlds, free from the troubles of old age and death, playing their dutiful roles in maintaining and managing the various aspects of creation as manifestations of the one Supreme God. Below them are a series of worlds, inhabited by different beings, with varying capabilities and celestial qualities, prone to destruction and mutation.

The ordinary mortals, which include human beings, live on earth and are subject to the cycle of births and deaths, the laws of karma and illusion. Below the earthly plane are some darker worlds where live dark and dangerous forces, pure evil, subject to wicked and egoistic impulses, whose primary task it is to oppose the divine forces and create terror and chaos in all the worlds including ours. They are actually the terrorists of the divine order who use their destructive and wicked powers to create fear and terror everywhere.

A constant battle between the gods and the demons goes on for supremacy of the heavens, while the greater gods, like the Trinity [Brahma, Shiva, and Vishnu], keep a benevolent watch upon the worlds and interfere if they feel that the quarrel between the two is becoming a bit too noisy for the worlds to bear with.

The fate of the divinities and the demons is almost fixed forever because their existence is rooted in the nature of their roles as the good and evil forces of the universe, while the mortal beings like us possess both the qualities and are capable of moving in either direction through the exercise of their individual wills and awareness. The divinities and the demons cannot actually evolve unless they come down to earth and subject themselves to our reality in physical form. Thus of all the beings in the universe, the mortals, and among mortals man, occupy an unique and enviable position that gives them a rare ability to evolve further and ascend into higher realms through their personal effort. When the demons succeed in creating chaos and anarchy in the worlds and when the divinities fail to contain them, they all beseech the higher gods to intervene and help them by restoring dharma and order. If the situation has really become serious and warrants intervention because some of the demons have become disproportionately strong and unbearably cruel, it results in the incarnation of Vishnu upon earth as a mortal being with a physical form to restore order, destroy evil and protect the good. This is known as incarnation of God. Sometimes instead of incarnating completely He incarnates partially either as a prophet, a saint or a sage to educate people on some finer aspects of religion or inspire them to follow the path of righteousness through his Messages.

Thus the Hindu pantheon is actually a schematic representation of the cosmic order in which various universal forces are organized and operate as part of the Divine Will, comprising God in His purest and Highest form, all His incarnations, emanations, manifestations, partial incarnations, with varying degress of energies and capabilities. Besides these, there are those who evolve themselves into higher divinities by virtue of their sheer effort and inner transformation. All these operate at various levels with varying degrees of qualities and energies. In essence and in their fundamental nature, they are illumined by the same Supreme Self. Because we cannot understand the concept of nonduality clearly without experiencing the oneness of creation, the difference whatever exists in our imagination and thinking.

Thus Hinduism is perhaps the only major religion in

the world with a credible theory of creation and a concept of reality characterized by an universal order managed and sustained by a rich variety of universal forces. It is our firm belief that by understanding them we can develop an insight into the way this universe is created, organized and managed by the Supreme God.

Since they play a positive and crucial role in maintaining the order of the universe that has a direct bearing upon our lives and activities and since we are inherently incapable of dealing with the problems of our existence entirely on our own, it makes perfect sense to worship them with sincere devotion and seek their help and guidance for our material and spiritual welfare. There is fundamentally no difference, whether we worship God as One or as Many as long as we worship Him with sincerity and devotion and are not causing trouble to others.

How the Gods Are Generally Worshipped

Over a period of time Hinduism evolved a diverse range of ritualistic worship of various gods and goddesses, characterized in many ways by the fundamental notion of God as the benefactor and bestower of boons who descends upon us and into our hearts and homes as a divine guest to shower his grace and benediction to the extent we are earnest and sincere in our faith and devotion. Complicated in many ways like the work of an artist or a scientist and seemingly naive and superstitious, they demand precision and perfection in their execution. Their efficacy depends upon the degree of sincerity, purity of purpose and the extent of devotion that go into their performance.

A standard form of Hindu ritualistic worship proceeds in the following manner. It begins with the invocation of a personal god (avahana) through prayers to draw his attention. Then he is welcomed into the house and to the place of worship where he is offered a high seat (asana). Once seated, the devotee washes his feet with sacred water (padya) and offers him a mixture of sandalwood paste and rice (arghya) as a mark of respect. A sacred thread of cotton (upavita) is put on the idol and sandalwood paste (chandana) is smeared once again to fill the place with a pleasant aroma. This is followed by the offering of flowers (pushpa), incense (dhupa), light (dipa), food (naivedya), betel leaves with nuts (tambula), camphor (nirajana), a gift of [a] golden flower (suvarnapushpa) and distribution of prasad or blessed food. At the end of the worship the idol is slightly moved and the deity is given a hearty farewell (visarjana). This in brief is the method of performing a Hindu puja which usually lasts anytime between five minutes to even five hours.

What Is the Nature of Worship in the Temples?

While the household worship of gods is built around the notion of God as the divine guest, that of temple worship revolves around the notion of God as the King and Emperor of this world who spends his time from morning till evening in the discharge of his kingly duties and in alleviating the suffering of his devotees. The process is more or less uniform in every temple, where the principal deity is treated like a divine emperor and attended upon with great sincerity and loyalty by the temple priests. Early in the morning, generally before sunrise, they wake him up to the accompaniment of music and devotional hymns, give him a bath, dress him up fully and gloriously and then worship him with all ardor and fervor making various offerings and chanting hymns of encomiums.

Thereupon he is worshipped and petitioned throughout the day by the priests as well as the visiting devotees with periods of rest in between till it is time for him to retire into his chambers with his consort. After preparing his bed and offering him the night meal, the priests lock the temple doors of the sanctum sanctorum [holy of holies] and retire to their houses to take rest while the god sleeps in his chambers. This process goes on day after day and throughout the year without break and the expenses for all this is borne by the temple administration supported either by its own sources of traditional income or donations from generous devotees. On some special occasions, such as festivals, an image of the temple deity which is specially meant for processions (utsvava murthy) is carried in a chariot or in palanquin through the main streets of the town or village where the temple is situated.

Is Idol Worship Justified?

The purpose of idol worship is not to perpetuate superstition, but to draw the people into religious life and thereby open their minds to divine thoughts. Idol worship is a very effective means of drawing the average minds towards the path of devotion who may not otherwise understand the concept of divine worship of a formless universal entity. By all means it is a good karma, better than wasting one's life and energies in meaningless pursuits that neither bring happiness nor develop character. It is a very convenient and natural means to communicate with God and contemplate upon God (bhagavad chintana) and relate ourselves to Him. Idol worship is better than religious hatred and persecution and discrimination in the name of religion. An idol worshipper has as much right to worship god as any and if he derives some meaning and satisfaction out of that why not? Any day, it is a better way of spending time than wasting our time in watching useless movies or indulging in worthless gossip!

Why Gods Allow the Destruction of Temples and Idols

Death and destruction are a part of this reality. Impermanence and change are very much the attributes of this mortal and unstable world. Nothing in this world is permanent and nothing really lasts including the name and form of God. An idol is not immortal, nor indestructible. It is a physical aspect of God, a form we create with our thoughts and emotions and bring it to life through our faith and devotion. It receives our love and attention because we perceive in it the ubiquitous presence of God. Whether it is destroyed by an act of nature or the insane act of man, should not make any difference to the faithful and the devoted. In many instances in Hinduism an idol is dissolved by the worshippers themselves after it is worshipped. What matters most in these matters is how strong our faith is and whether it withstands the impact of delusion. As long as our faith is not broken, it does not matter what happens in this world including our human notions of God.

It is important to note that God is not vengeful and would not stop evil from doing what it wants to do. God would not draw a sword against evil for our benefit and amusement. God helps both good and evil to enact their drama in this world of illusion. He fulfills the wishes of both, according to their faith, as is evident from many stories from the Hindu mythology. (In many instances He granted boons to devoted demons, who were highly destructive.) What is more important in such matter is how strong your faith is and how much trust you can repose in God despite all the evil that goes on in this world. . . .

Representing the Female Part of the Divine

Saraswathi

Saraswathi is the goddess of learning. She is extolled in the Vedas as the sacred river with seven sisters, who helps the gods by destroying their foes. The early Vedic Aryans worshipped not the Ganges, but the Saraswathi river, which is mentioned several times in the Rigveda, while there is no specific reference to the river Ganges. Saraswathi river used to flow in western India through what is now the Thar desert. It dried up eventually with changes in the climate.

Saraswathi actually means "the one who flows". Saraswathi is a river of knowledge that flows in the highest heavens of Brahma and descends into our minds through the doors of learning to become established in us through self effort. She is worshipped by all students. Saraswathi grants wisdom, knowledge, creativity and intuition for the flowering of our minds and refinement of our character. Saraswathi is vagdevi, speech personified. Speech is central to our lives and activities on earth. It also distinguishes us from [the] rest of the animal kingdom. Speech was also at the root of all Sanskrit mantras and religious activity. One can therefore understand the

importance of this divinity in [the] Hindu pantheon.
Saraswathi is the goddess of light who dispels our ignorance and inner darkness through her grace. Even
gods worship her for developing proficiency in different fields. She is addressed with different names by her
devotees. Sarada (giver of essence), Vagesvari (controller of speech), Bharathi, Kalavathi, Brahmi (consort
of Brahma) and Veenadhari (holder of the Veena) are
some of her most popular names.

She is generally depicted as a beautiful and graceful
goddess in spotless white clothes, seated on a lotus seat,
holding a Veena [stringed instrument] on her lap or in
her hand, with a beautiful peacock or a swan wandering
nearby, probably enjoying the celestial music coming
from her. In her images, she is shown with four hands,
holding a Veena, a book, a rosary and lotus respectively.
These objects sometimes vary, but they generally sym-
bolize her connection with learning and knowledge.
Her vehicle is generally either a swan or a peacock. The
swan symbolizes beauty, grace and wisdom, while the
peacock symbolizes the same in addition to its ability to
deal with desires and ignorance (snakes). . . .

Lakshmi

Lakshmi is the consort of Mahavishnu, the resplendent
goddess of wealth and provider of all material comforts,
who was born from the milky ocean when the gods and
demons churned it in search of ambrosia and was pre-
sented to Vishnu as a gift. She is generally shown seated
on a lotus flower holding lotus flowers in two hands
while the other two remain in abhaya (assurance) and
varada (giving) mudras (gestures) respectively. Two elephants stand on either side spraying water through

their raised trunks. Sometimes she is shown in the company of Mahavishnu and sometimes showering gold coins upon her devotees. The owl is her vehicle. . . . The owl stands symbolically for intelligence, ill omen or bad luck and an unusual life style characterized by loneliness and fear which are also interestingly the companions of the rich and famous.

Lakshmi has many aspects which generally correspond [to] the various forms of wealth. Tradition recognizes eight forms collectively known as Ashtalakshmis (eight Lakshmis), each representing a particular type of wealth, namely: Adilakshmi (First), Dhanyalakshmi (crops), Dhairyalakshmi (courage), Gajalakshmi (elephants), Santanalakshmi (children), Vijayalakshmi (victory), Vidyalakshmi (education), and Dhanalakshmi (riches).

Incarnations of Lakshmi: Whenever Mahavishnu incarnates on earth in a human form, Lakshmi incarnates along with Him and plays her part in restoring Dharma. She incarnated as Padma when Vishnu incarnated upon earth as Vamana, as Dharani when he incarnated as Parasurama, as Sita when he incarnated as Rama and as Rukmini when he incarnated as Krishna.

Lakshmi is worshipped during [the] Diwali festival by most Hindus with a lot of fanfare. Traditionally Indian businessmen, merchants and traders, open their annual account books after worshipping her in their offices and business establishments on this occasion. . . .

Parvathi

Parvathi is the consort of Siva [Shiva]. She got her name because she is the daughter of the mountains (parvatha) and also because she as Prakriti occupies one half (parva) of the universe while the other half is occupied by Siva in his aspect as Iswara or Purusha. She is known by many names and worshipped by many both as a consort of Siva and also independently as the Mother Goddess. We do not come across any direct reference to her in the Rigveda, but in the Kenopanishad [a later text] she is mentioned as Uma Haimavathi, the daughter of Himavat, who declares to the gods the greatness of Brahman.

According to Hindu mythology Parvathi was Dakshayani in her previous incarnation. Dakshayani was the daughter of Daksha and Prasuti. She became the wife of Siva much against her father's wishes. The story is that Daksha once perform[ed] a sacrifice and invite[d] all gods to grace the occasion. During the ceremony, in front [of] every one he speaks insultingly about Siva who has not been invited to attend the function. Unable to bear the insult to her husband, Dakshayani immolates herself in front of every one. In her next birth she is born again as Parvathi and through her austerities and penances she wins over Siva and marries him again.

Parvathi is generally shown seated by the side of her husband or in the company of her children and husband. She is also shown separately as a Shakti, seated on a pedestal, or a lion or a tiger with four hands and a cheerful face. Two of her hands hold lotus flowers while the remaining two are in the abhaya and varada mudras (postures). Parvathi is also known by many other names such as Uma, Amba or Ambika and Gauri.

Brahmi, Mahesvari, Kaumari, Vaisnavi, Vahahi, Narasimhi and Aindri are considered [to] be the seven manifestations of Kali, who is Parvathi in her terrible form. These goddesses were actually created by the combined energies of seven different gods (Brahman, Siva, Kumara, Vishnu, Varaha) who wanted to help Kali who was fighting Raktabija, a powerful demon. These goddesses display the basic attributes of the gods from which they descended and also carry the same weapons as their counterparts. . . .

Durga is the Mother Goddess aspect of Parvathi. A whole lot of tradition is associated with her, which goes back to the prevedic period. The Devibhagavatham, a purana [sacred story], is entirely dedicated to her. So is the case with Devimahatyam, also known as Durgasaptasathi. Durga is the Mother of all, universal love personified, who is considered by her followers to be superior to even the Trinity. She slew the demon Mahishasura, the bull-headed demon who was troubling all the worlds and whom no god was able to fight.

Riding on a ferocious lion, holding innumerable weapons, and with several hands, she fought the demon and put an end to him. The festival Dussehara, one of the most popular Hindu festivals, is observed to celebrate the victory of good over the evil. Because of this victory, Durga is also called Mahishasuramardini (slayer of Mahisha). She also slew several demons, like Chanda and Munda, Sumbha and Nisumbha and earned her reputation as [a] terror to all the evil in the universe.

Durga as the controller of the universe and the Highest Self has a trinity of her own represented by Mahasarasvathi, Mahalakshmi and Mahakali. They are not counterparts to Brahma, Vishnu and Mahesh, but considered by her worshippers as the Trinity Itself, representing the creative, preservative and destructive aspects of Durga as Iswari or Mahadevi.

Durga has many aspects some of which we have already mentioned while dealing with the aspects of Parvathi. Mahakali is her most terrible aspect. Mahakali is a ferocious goddess, dark blue in color, with ten faces and feet, with a garland of skulls or slain heads dangling around her neck, her hands holding various kinds of destructive weapons, with one foot resting on the body of a fallen Siva. . . .

Two Popular Gods

Ganesha

Ganesha is the leader of the Sivaganas (the forces of Siva). He is the first among the gods to receive all the honors. He is called Vighnaraja, lord of the obstacles and impediments. Devout Hindus worship him for removal of obstacles. Before starting any particular venture or worshipping other gods, they remember Ganesha, their beloved god. The only exception to this rule is when Siva is worshipped. Siva is the father of Ganesha. When you worship the father there is no need to worship the son separately because the son is always found in the heart of his father. So when Siva is worshipped Ganesha is kept in the sidelines.

Of all the gods, Ganesha attracts and arrests our attention. No one can fail to notice his peculiar features and his unusual placement in the Hindu pantheon. Looking at his form, a foreigner, who is not familiar with the tenets of Hinduism, would perhaps draw wrong conclusions about Ganesha and about Hinduism.

But he would be surprised to know that despite his looks, Ganesha is one of the most popular gods of Hinduism. Irrespective of their age, gender, education and background, millions are drawn to him irresistibly and worship him deeply with unparallel[ed] devotion. His very presence adds a lot of variety and vibrancy to Hinduism. His childlike innocence and behavior, attract the younger lot and draw them into religious life from an early age. They develop [a] friendship with Ganesha and that friendship stays with them for the remainder of their lives.

Ganesha has a peculiar, if not grotesque form. His form defies all norms of physical beauty and sense of proportion. But it does not invoke any sense of ugliness or repulsion in those who are devoted to him. Filled with love in their hearts, they see in him a peculiar charm, that is uniquely his own and powerfully appealing. He is short in stature, almost dwarfish to look at and red in color. Circumstances made him live with an elephant head, which sits rather confidently on a big pot belly supported by the stout limbs and legs of a sumo warrior. The color of his body is usually red. But his images in blue, black, green, yellow, white or pink colors are available.

He lost one of his tusks in an encounter with Parasurama. So he is left with only one which we see in all his images. The other tusk sometimes appears in his hand and serves as his pen. He is shown with four arms, seated or standing. Sometimes we see more than four hands. Each arm holds a different object. A snake girdles around his pot belly and a yajnopavitam (a sacred thread) dangles across his shoulders. Sometimes the sacred thread is substituted with a snake.

He also wears a golden or a silver crown. Rarely we see him with long and flowing hair. A large sivanama adorns his forehead, with a third eye in the middle. His trunk may be turned to the left or to the right, depending upon your luck and the intentions of the artist or the sculptor who makes the image. A small funny looking mouse serves him as his vehicle. Looking at the mouse one wonders whether it is his vehicle or his pet, for the mouse hardly seems to have been put to work. One can see it happily sitting at the feet of its master and nibbling away at the tasty food served to its master.

The mystery behind his form: Despite his looks and abnormal form, Ganesha has millions of followers and devotees all over the world. This amply illustrates the point that true devotion to God independent of our mental notions of form and beauty and that men are capable of worshipping God in all his manifestations, irrespective of what he appears to be.

Ganesha has a peculiar beauty and charm of his own. His is not a surface beauty. Hidden behind his peculiar features is a far deeper harmony which a casual glance fails to notice. As you become his true devotee and open your heart to his love, you realize his truly radiant personality. When he touches your heart, you see in Him the beauty of true innocence, purity, divinity and a childlike consciousness that touches your heart with all its captivating charm and ever flowing tenderness. No other god brings out the child in you with all the associated feelings as Ganesha does. No other god, with the sole exception of perhaps his parents, invokes in you the combined feelings of awe and fear. Those who have true devotion to him are able to experience these emotions and understand his true significance.

He is known by many names. The most popular ones include: Ganapathi (lord of the ganas), Vighneswara (lord of the obstacles), Lambodara (potbellied), Vakrathunda (with a curved trunk), Mahaganapathi (great Ganapathi), Parvathinandana (son of Parvathi), Mushikavahana (rider of a mouse), Ekadantaya (one with one tusk), Kumaraguru (child guru), Siddhivinayaka (boon giver), and Balaganapathi (child Ganapathi). There are many other names and forms. There is no temple in India, old or new, without an image of Ganesha in the temple precincts. . . .

Hanuman

Hanuman is one of the most popular gods of Hinduism. People from all [walks] of life worship him and admire him. As a devotee of Lord Rama, he has become very popular for his devotion and great qualities. Like Ganesha he commands respect and veneration from children and elders alike. Any one who is familiar with the Ramayana, cannot but appreciate his divine nature and super human personality, shaped by the strength of celibacy, humility, selflessness, unsurpassed devotion, determination, fearlessness and an extraordinary commitment to work for the divine.

His temples are found everywhere in India, in towns and cities, on the hills, in the forests and most difficult places. Millions observe [a] fast on Tuesdays and refrain from drinking and smoking as a mark of respect for him. Sita [Rama's consort] found in him a friend, a son and a loyal servant. Impressed by his loyalty and commitment to the cause of Rama, she blessed him to remain immortal in his existing form till the end of creation and help the loyal devotees of Rama.

People believe that he is very much active on earth even today. . . . People pray to him for courage and confidence, freedom from sorrow and for protection against evil spirits and bad luck. Hanuman is a terror to evil forces. Because of his intense purity and devotion they are afraid to appear anywhere near him.

When people pray to Hanuman, they generally chant

the chalisa for boons and protection. The chalisa is a verse of 40 lines containing pure adulation. It describes the great qualities and adventures of Hanuman. It is said that because of his complete humility he would not stir into action, unless one reminds him of his true greatness and his divine purpose. His devotees therefore chant the chalisa, to remind him of his greatness and prompt him to wake up from his devotion and help them. Hanuman's chalisa has become a modern mantra, more popular, perhaps, than the Ramacharitamanas itself. Many of his devotees may not know Hindi. But they would chant chalisa with sincerity and faith.

In appearance Hanuman looks like a well built monkey with the strength of a gorilla. His gait is very much human, despite his monkey features, and he conducts himself admirably, without the clumsy movements of an ape. Physically he is half human and half monkey. He probably came from a race that had become extinct. Hanuman lives in the hearts of people through his exemplary devotion and surrender to God. Physically he is endowed with unlimited powers. Being the son of Vayu, the wind god, he has the ability to increase or decrease his size at will and also fly into the air and travel to far away regions of the earth and the solar system.

In the imagery of Rama, we generally see Hanuman, standing reverentially on a side, sitting or standing in a humble manner with his hands joined in reverence. When he is shown alone, he appears in different ways, sitting cross legged, kneeling, standing or flying. In all cases we see him holding his weapon, the mace. When he is shown as flying in the air like a superman, he carries a mountain with one hand and the mace with the other. In some temples we see very tall and imposing images of Hanuman reminding us of his immense strength.

The Tenth Teaching of the Bhagavad Gita

from the Bhagavad Gita

The following selection is from the Bhagavad Gita, Hinduism's most central text. Even Jawaharlal Nehru, India's first prime minister and a man who claimed little interest in religion, kept a copy of the Gita at his bedside. The text's author is unknown, and scholars generally accept that it was inserted into the *Mahabharata*, a great epic poem of ancient India, in the first century A.D. The *Mahabharata*, the bulk of which dates from centuries earlier, concerns clan conflicts and religious struggles from the period around 1000 B.C. when Aryan migrants conquered north India. The Bhagavad Gita fits within this context, taking place at the side of a field that is to be the site of a major battle. Arjuna, a Kshatriya (warrior) caste Hindu, expresses concerns that he might be called upon to kill members of his family and teachers he admires in the coming fight, and he wonders how such action could be good. The remainder of the text is a dialogue between the hesitant Arjuna and the god Krishna, who takes the form of Arjuna's charioteer. In the following Tenth Teaching, Krishna reminds Arjuna that, despite his current form, he is the godhead, known by many names and all powerful. It is not, claims Krishna in other teachings, for

Barbara Stoler Miller, translator, *The Bhagavad-Gita: Krishna's Counsel in Time of War*. New York: Columbia University Press, 1986. Copyright © 1986 by Columbia University Press. Reproduced by permission.

men and women to question their earthly roles but to
take action, in war for instance, and in so doing
achieve a greater spiritual understanding.

Lord Krishna
Great Warrior, again hear
my word in its supreme form;
desiring your good,
I speak to deepen your love.

Neither the multitude of gods
nor great sages know my origin,
for I am the source of all
the gods and great sages.

A mortal who knows me
as the unborn, beginningless
great lord of the worlds
is freed from delusion and all evils.

Understanding, knowledge, nondelusion,
patience, truth, control, tranquility,
joy, suffering, being, nonbeing,
fear, and fearlessness. . . .

Nonviolence, equanimity, contentment,
penance, charity, glory, disgrace,
these diverse attitudes
of creatures' arise from me.

The seven ancient great sages
and the four ancestors of man
are mind-born aspects of me;
their progeny fills the world.

The man who in reality knows
my power and my discipline
is armed with unwavering discipline;
in this there is no doubt.

I am the source of everything;
and everything proceeds from me;
filled with my existence, wise men
realizing this are devoted to me.

Thinking and living deep in me,
they enlighten one another
by constantly telling of me
for their own joy and delight.

To men of enduring discipline,
devoted to me with affection,
I give the discipline of understanding
by which they come to me.

Dwelling compassionately
deep in the self,
I dispel darkness born of ignorance
with the radiant light of knowledge.

Arjuna
You are supreme, the infinite spirit,
the highest abode, sublime purifier,
man's spirit, eternal, divine,
the primordial god, unborn, omnipotent.

So the ancient seers spoke of you,
as did the epic poet Vyasa and the bards
who sang for gods, ancestors, and men;
and now you tell me yourself.

Lord Krishna, I realize the truth

of all you tell me;
neither gods nor demons
know your manifest nature.

You know yourself through the self,
Krishna; Supreme among Men,
Sustainer and Lord of Creatures,
God of Gods, Master of the Universe!

Tell me without reserve
the divine powers of your self,
powers by which you pervade
these worlds.

Lord of Discipline,
how can I know you as I meditate
on you—in what diverse aspects
can I think of you, Krishna?

Recount in full extent
the discipline and power of your self;
Krishna, I can never hear enough
of your immortal speech.

Lord Krishna
Listen, Arjuna, as I recount
for you in essence
the divine powers of my self;
endless is my extent.

I am the self abiding
in the heart of all creatures;
I am their beginning,
their middle, and their end.

I am Vishnu striding among sun gods,
the radiant sun among lights;

I am lightning among wind gods,
the moon among the stars.

I am the song in sacred lore;
I am Indra, king of the gods;
I am the mind of the senses,
the consciousness of creatures.

I am gracious Shiva among howling storm gods,
the lord of wealth among demigods and demons,
fire blazing among the bright gods;
I am golden Meru towering over the mountains.

Arjuna, know me as the gods' teacher,
chief of the household priests;
I am the god of war among generals;
I am the ocean of lakes.

I am Bhrigu, priest of the great seers;
of words, I am the eternal syllable OM,
the prayer of sacrifices;
I am Himalaya, the measure of what endures.

Among trees, I am the sacred fig-tree;
I am chief of the divine sages,
leader of the celestial musicians,
the recluse philosopher among saints.

Among horses, know me as the immortal stallion
born from the sea of elixir;
among elephants, the divine king's mount,
among men, the king.

I am the thunderbolt among weapons,
among cattle, the magical wish-granting cow;
I am the procreative god of love,
the king of the snakes.

I am the endless cosmic serpent,
the lord of all sea creatures;
I am chief of the ancestral fathers;
of restraints, I am death.

I am the pious son of demons;
of measures, I am time;
I am the lion among wild animals,
the eagle among birds.

I am the purifying wind,
the warrior Rama bearing arms,
the sea-monster crocodile,
the flowing river Ganges.

I am the beginning, the middle,
and the end of creations, Arjuna;
of sciences, I am the science of the self;
I am the dispute of orators.

I am the vowel *a* of the syllabary,
the pairing of words in a compound;
I am indestructible time,
the creator facing everywhere at once.

I am death the destroyer of all,
the source of what will be,
the feminine powers: fame, fortune, speech,
memory, intelligence, resolve, patience.

I am the great ritual chant,
the meter of sacred song,
the most sacred month in the year,
the spring blooming with flowers.

I am the dice game of gamblers,
the brilliance of fiery heroes.

I am victory and resolve,
the lucidity of lucid men.

I am Krishna among my mighty kinsmen;
I am Arjuna among the Pandava princes;
I am the epic poet Vyasa among sages,
the inspired singer among bards.

I am the scepter of rulers,
the morality of ambitious men;
I am the silence of mysteries,
what men of knowledge know.

Arjuna, I am the seed
of all creatures;
nothing animate or inanimate
could exist without me.

Fiery Hero, endless
are my divine powers—
of my power's extent
I have barely hinted.

Whatever is powerful, lucid,
splendid, or invulnerable
has its source in a fragment
of my brilliance.

What use is so much knowledge
to you, Arjuna?
I stand sustaining this entire world
with a fragment of my being.

Hinduism Outside India: The Island of Bali

by Ian Grant

Although Hinduism is practiced all around the world by expatriate populations of Indians, it is the main religion of only two places: the modern nation of India and the island of Bali in the Indonesian archipelago. The following selection is a description of certain Balinese Hindu practices. The author, Ian Grant, notes that Balinese Hindus share with Indian Hindus reverence for such texts as the *Ramayana*, belief in such gods as Shiva and Vishnu, and a conception of caste as a basis for both social and religious organization.

During the centuries from A.D. 200 to 800 Indian customs spread southward and eastward via trade and migration, producing what one scholar called the "Indianized states of Southeast Asia" in regions stretching from modern-day Myanmar to Cambodia and south through Thailand and Malaysia to Indonesia. Hinduism was a component of this cultural exchange, and Hindu beliefs informed the construction of such well-known monuments as Angkor Wat, built in Cambodia in the twelfth century, and Borobudur, built on the main Indonesian island of Java beginning in the eighth century. Bali itself is dotted with ancient temples. Much of Southeast Asia in time converted to either Buddhism or Islam, although religious mixing proved the norm and aspects of Hinduism remained important even in Buddhist or Muslim areas. Versions of the *Ramayana*, for instance, continued to be revered in Buddhist countries. As Grant notes below, the most important form of religious interchange, at least in Bali, was between Hinduism and earlier beliefs and customs. Ian Grant is a New Zealand author who also serves on the board of the Auckland University of Technology.

For convenience Bali's religion has been labelled Hindu. And it is true that *gamelans* [groups of Balinese musicians] dramatically accent Rama's heroic rescue of his bride Sita from the terrible giant Rawana, that fearsome warriors and noble princes from the same *Ramayana* legends crowd *batik* designs. But in the same way that Hindu mythology simply added more colour to existing artforms, fifteenth-century Javanese-Hinduism was only the last of a succession of religions to be absorbed into the belief system of the inquisitive and acquisitive Balinese.

At bottom, beneath a scholar's nightmare of freely-adapted beliefs that can be traced to several Hindu cults and several more Buddhist sects, the Balinese are ancestor-worshipping animists, who see everything as manifestations of good or evil.

Caste in Bali

The Hindu heritage is perhaps strongest in the island's social system. This, in fact, is closer to ancient Vedic beliefs than India's rigid caste system. There are four castes on Bali, but no outcastes. Caste determines whom a man may marry, but it does not influence his choice of occupation or friends, whereas in India there is an actual and unbridgable gulf between the castes.

In Bali the differences are symbolic. Caste is essentially a prestige system. High and low caste Balinese will sit cross-legged together and play in the same *gamelan*. But the nobleman will make sure he is sitting at a slightly higher level than the lower-caste *sudra*. He will speak to his companion in the everyday Malay language of the marketplace and the *sudra* will be expected to struggle with a language of Sanskrit-Javanese origin and its flowery speech-patterns.

The *sudras*, who form 90 per cent of the population, accept the divine superiority of the three noble castes. These descendants of the Madjapahit Javanese, with resounding titles of little political substance, have cleverly assured their superior status by claiming Hindu gods as family ancestors. To the Balinese peasant, however, his own ancestral gods are more important than the abstract and alien Brahma, Shiva and Vishna. The protecting ancestral gods must be served diligently and, when necessary, evil spirits must be frightened away with magic and witchcraft.

From birth to death, life on Bali is an extended religious act. The 210-day Balinese year is crammed with ceremonies and festivals. Some are conducted privately behind the mud walls that surround house courtyards, some are celebrated in village temples, and others are great feast days throughout Bali.

Mixed Hindu and Local Practices

With several generations in each family courtyard, life-cycle ceremonies follow one another in endless procession. A husband will make offerings at the family shrine during his wife's pregnancy because he wants a son. When the son is born he will thank the ancestral spirits for their part in ensuring the continuation of the family line. He may also congratulate himself for buying, at the sacrifice of several glasses of potent *arak* spirit, magic charms to scare away the *leyaks*, troublesome witches who feed on the blood of pregnant women.

It seems ironic to the outsider that the life ambition of every Balinese should be an elaborate cremation. The Balinese believe that the ceremonial burning of the corpse liberates its soul, setting it free for higher and higher reincarnations.

Cremations are neither private or solemn: whole *banjars* [village associations] help with preparations and join in the joyful, carnival-like ceremonies. Traditionally, cremations were so costly that they sometimes ruined wealthy princes. The soul of one deceased raja [prince] was released to the accompaniment of one hundred and twenty-six *gamelans*. Peasants were often forced to wait years before cremating what little remained of their dead, haunted by the belief that, unless a soul was liberated, it would one day return to the family compound as a malevolent ghost.

Today, with the economic consequences of population pressure felt by all Balinese, elaborate cremations have become rare. But occasionally a prince will make a brave attempt to halt the steady decline in his prestige, and will cremate a relative in the old style.

A Royal Cremation

The theatrical effects produced by the sun before sliding over the horizon, turning shadows deep purple and grass a shade of blue, set the scene perfectly. There is a stirring, a murmuring, and then a shouting as groups of men struggle in the palace's ceremonial gateway for possession of the white-shrouded body. One group breaks away and rushes the corpse across the square to the *wadah* or cremation tower, glittering with a thousand tiny mirrors. The soul has already left its body, so the white bundle is roughly pushed and dragged up the tottering, pagoda-roofed, bamboo tower to a small platform a dizzy height above the crowd.

An abstracted Brahmin priest is helped on to the lowest platform already crowded with musicians. Then a hundred men heave the tower on to their shoulders. The soft music of the shadowplay can scarcely be heard as the shouting mob of bearers rushes in and out of the procession heading for the cremation ground. At every crossroad the pitching, swaying, sixty-foot tower is whirled in gigantic circles to confuse the evil spirits.

At the cremation ground the corpse is transferred to the sarcophagus, a bull-shaped coffin. The bull stands in a gaily decorated pavilion, its hollow tree-trunk body dressed with velvet, silk and beaten silver. The pyre is lit and flames dart up the animal's flanks. At last, its legs buckle and the proud head drops into the fire.

The sun is setting when ashes gathered from the smouldering coffin are carried to the seashore in another procession. The priest wades chest-high into the sea and sprinkles the ashes into water reflecting an enormous, scarlet moon. The *wadahs* are all set on fire. They burn fiercely and crash to the ground, then the musicians play the weary procession home to its village.

There are thousands of temples on Bali. There are temples on the slopes of sacred mountains, in village and town squares, in the middle of ricefields, even along

Traditional architectural features are evident in this gateway to a Balinese Hindu temple in Besakih.

the island's rugged coastline. And every single temple celebrates annually the anniversary of its founding.

Some temples are dedicated to the Hindu pantheon of gods, some to the goddesses of learning, rice or fertility, but most provide, like the simplest family shrines, a resting-place for the ancestral spirits when they visit their descendants.

Temple Rites and Festivals

All Balinese temples look as if they were built from the same ancient architectural blueprint. A split gate leads into the first of two low-walled, open-air courtyards. This court, with its cooking and orchestra sheds, is a kind of antechamber. Steps climb up to a second gate identical to the first except that the two halves now form one massive structure, with only the narrowest opening into the temple proper. There are no idols, but shrines and altars where gods rest during their earthly visits. Most elaborate are the *merus*, wooden pagodas with sugar-palm roofs which may be built eleven stories high.

Between festivals a temple is silent, deserted except for the *pemanekus* or village priests who occasionally sweep away the leaves and palm fronds that quickly cover the courtyards. But once a year the temple is a living part of the community. The shrines are decorated, the stone demons guarding the inner courtyard wear jaunty red hibiscus blooms behind their ears, the temple fills with a great, rowdy festival crowd.

A temple anniversary, perhaps at the Temple of the Ancestors or even the Temple of the Dead, is the whole village's business. The finest chefs, virtuosi like their brother artists in illustrious European hotels, roast sucking pig and sea-turtles and season them with pungent spices. With instinctive design and colour sense, and an uncanny grasp of basic architectural principles, women build fruit, flowers and cakes into perfectly symmetrical pyramid-shaped temple offerings that are often six feet high. The twenty-seven musicians in the *gong gede*, the *gamelan* equivalent of a full symphony orchestra, nonchalantly beat out the stately, tranquil temple melodies they have been practising for weeks.

Islamic Challenges to Hinduism

by Octavio Paz

Although most of the more than 1 billion people living in modern India are Hindus, greater than 100 million are Muslims. In earlier periods, before the Indian subcontinent was partitioned into India proper and the two mostly Muslim nations of Pakistan and Bangladesh, the Islamic proportion of the region's population was even larger than the approximately 10 percent it is today. For nearly one thousand years Hindus and Muslims have lived side by side. In fact, from approximately 1200 to 1757, most of India was governed by Islamic emperors such as the Moguls who built the Taj Mahal and other famous monuments.

The following selection is by Nobel Prize–winning Mexican writer Octavio Paz, who served as his country's ambassador to India for six years in the 1960s after a brief earlier stint as an attaché. He describes the historical interaction between Hindus and Muslims, noting that, among other factors, Islam was particularly appealing to low-caste Hindus seeking freedom from caste restrictions. Paz also discusses the influences that Islam, particularly in its mystical Sufi form, likely had on Hinduism. One result of the combination of the two faiths was the so-called bhakti, or devotional, sect of Hinduism, which was common in South India in the centuries before 1500 and which resulted in some of the greatest Hindu poetry. Bhakti focused on the common love of the divine, or of "god," which could take various forms, including the great Hindu gods Shiva and Vishnu as well as the Islamic Allah. The movement failed, Paz notes, to create a lasting bridge between two very different religions.

———————————

The first thing that surprised me about India, as it has surprised so many others, was the diversity created by extreme contrast: modernity and antiquity, luxury and poverty, sensuality and asceticism, carelessness and efficiency, gentleness and violence; a multiplicity of castes and languages, gods and rites, customs and ideas, rivers and deserts, plains and mountains, cities and villages, rural and industrial life, centuries apart in time and neighbors in space. But the most remarkable aspect of India, and the one that defines it, is neither political nor economic, but religious: the coexistence of Hinduism and Islam. The presence of the strictest and most extreme form of monotheism alongside the richest and most varied polytheism is, more than a historical paradox, a deep wound. Between Islam and Hinduism there is not only an opposition, but an incompatibility. In one, the theology is rigid and simple; in the other, the variety of doctrines and sects induces a kind of vertigo. A minimum of rites among the Muslims; a proliferation of ceremonies among the Hindus. Hinduism is a conjunction of complicated rituals, while Islam is a clear and simple faith. Islamic monotheism categorically affirms the preeminence of the One: one God, one doctrine, and one brotherhood of believers. Of course, Islam has experienced divisions within itself, but these have been neither as profound nor as numerous as those within Hinduism, which accepts not only a plurality of gods but also of doctrines (*darshanas*), sects, and congregations of believers. Some of these brotherhoods of believers—true religions themselves within the great pluralistic religion of Hinduism—approach Christian monotheism; for example, among the followers of Krishna. Others recall the original polytheism of the Indo-Europeans: worshiping deities who are the guardians of cosmic order, warrior gods, and gods of agriculture and commerce. In one case, a creator god; in the other, the wheel of successive cosmic eras with its procession of gods and civilizations.

The great religious, poetic, legal, and historical books of the Hindus could not be more different from those of the Indian Muslims; nor is there anything similar in their architectural, artistic, and literary styles. Are they two civilizations occupying a single territory, or are they two religions nurtured by a single civilization? It is impossible to say. Hinduism began in India, and it holds an intimate and filial relation with the Vedic religion of the Aryan tribes who settled in the subcontinent in the second millennium before Christ. In contrast, Islam is a religion that came from abroad fully formed, with a theology to which nothing could be added. It came, moreover, as the faith of the foreign armies who, beginning in the eighth century, invaded India. Islam was imposed, but it took root in India and has remained the religion of millions for a thousand years. Despite these centuries of living side by side, the two communities have preserved their separate identities; there has been no fusion of the two. Nevertheless, many things unite them: similar customs, languages, love of the land, cuisine, music, popular art, clothing, and—to cut short a list that could become interminable—history. A history that unites them but also separates them. They have lived together, but their coexistence has been one of rivalry, full of suspicions, threats, and silent resentments that frequently have turned into bloodshed.

Islam Enters Hindu India

The first forays of Muslim soldiers into India were in the year 712, in the province of Sind. These began as looting expeditions but quickly turned into a full-scale invasion. After the occupation of the Punjab, the Sultanate of Delhi was founded in 1206. Until its disappearance in the sixteenth century, it was ruled by various dynasties, all of them of Turkish origin. These conquerors and their descendants left the social fabric almost entirely intact, so that life in the villages and hamlets barely changed. In the cities, however, the ancient ruling groups—Brahmans, Kshatriyas, wealthy merchants—were replaced by a new, Turkish aristocracy. It was a religious, political, and economic upheaval, the consequence of a military victory, but one that did not affect the basic social structures, although many people converted to Islam. The political position of the sultans was a maintenance of the status quo, as the population generally remained Hindu; the conversion by sword, urged by the orthodox, would have led to social chaos. At the same time, the sultans and the nobility [in the words of Muslim historian S.M. Ikram,] "always sought to conserve their position of dominance not only over the natives who were not Muslim, but also over the Indians who had adopted the Islamic faith as well as the Muslim Turks who had come from distant regions."

The Delhi Sultanate, though wracked by internecine struggles and the rebellions of ambitious nobles, was the center of the entire Muslim world. Its flourishing coincided with a period of Islamic decadence, and with the catastrophe that ended the Caliphate: the sack of Baghdad by Genghiz Khan's troops in 1258. Many Muslim intellectuals and artists sought refuge in the new capital. Yet, [according to S.M. Ikram in *Muslim Civilization in India*] "despite the cultural eminence of [Delhi], it cannot be claimed that the Sultanate is a period marked by that solid scholarship and study of the sciences which distinguished Baghdad and Cordoba." In essence, Delhi never had an Averroës or an Avicenna [two great Islamic thinkers]. The great creative period of Islam was over. This is one of the historical paradoxes of Muslim India: it flourished at the decline of Islamic civilization. There were, of course, poets of great distinction, such as Amir Khusrau, who wrote in Persian and in Hindi, and important Muslim works of history, a genre practically unknown in Hindu literature. Perhaps even more significant, from the point of view of the relations between the Hindu and Muslim cultures, was music. It is well known that Indian music deeply influenced that of the Arab world and central Asia. Music was one of the things that united the two communities. Exactly the opposite occurred with architecture and painting. Compare Ellora with the Taj Mahal, or the frescoes of Ajanta with Mughal miniatures [Ellora and Ajanta are classical Hindu monuments; the Taj Mahal, of the Islamic Mogul (Mughal) Empire (1526–1757)]. These are not distinct artistic styles, but rather two different visions of the world.

As for the conversion of the natives, almost all of the millions who adopted the new faith came from the lower castes. The phenomenon may be explained as the result of three circumstances: first, the new political and military order after the conquest; second, the possibility offered by Islam for one to free oneself from the chain of birth and rebirth (the terrible law of *karma*), a liberation that was not only religious but also social: the converted became part of a fraternity of believers; third, the work of the Muslim missionaries. The Sufis zealously preached in the two areas that today are ruled by officially Islamic states: Pakistan and Bangladesh. In Sufi mysticism there is a pantheistic vein that has certain affinities with Hinduism. During the Delhi Sultanate, between the thirteenth and fourteenth centuries, three Sufi orders emigrated to India. Its members had a profound influence among the Muslims as well as among the Hindus; many of the former adopted the pantheistic monism of the Hindu poets and mystics: all is God, and to unite with all is to unite with God. A doctrine clearly heretical for orthodox Islam, which has maintained that between God and his creatures there is an uncrossable abyss. The conflict between the orthodoxy (*Sharī'a*) and Sufi mysticism has deeply marked Islamic religious literature. Its case is not unique: there was a similar tension between the Roman Catholic Church and the mystical movements of Western Christianity, from St. Francis of Assisi to St. John of the Cross.

Bhakti Devotion: A Possible Middle Way

The Sufi tradition, during the Delhi Sultanate, is rich in important figures, such as the famous saint Nīzam uddin, who is still venerated in a mausoleum in Delhi that also contains the remains of Amir Khusrau, his friend. But although the Sufism of that period did not transgress the limits of orthodoxy, the end of the Sultanate also marked a fusion of Hindu and Sufi mysticism. Among the Hindus, there was a movement of popular devotion to a personal god (*bhakti*). For the believer, this personal deity incarnates the Absolute, and to unite with this god is to reach liberation (*moksha*), or at least to experience the joy of the divine. Not surprisingly, this popular devotion became the source, throughout India, of poems, songs, and dances. But it is poor in philosophical and theological speculation, the opposite of the Brahmanic tradition. In bhakti one reaches the divine not through reason but through love. The three gods whom these sects worshiped were Vishnu, Shiva, and Devi, the great goddess in her various manifestations. The cult of Vishnu, in turn, had two forms: devotion to Krishna or to Rāma, both avatars of the same god.

In these movements in which pantheism blended with the cult of a personal god, it is possible to recognize certain traces of Sufism. The great difference, in my opinion, is that bhakti, although as full of affection and love for God as Sufism, is an impure, a relative, monotheism. Becoming one with Krishna or with the Goddess, the devotee unites with a manifestation of the Absolute, not with a creator God. Krishna is not a unique god, exclusive of others, as Allah is in Islam. Nevertheless, the affirmation that the road to God is neither through ritual, the axis of Hinduism, nor through understanding, the basis of all the darshanas, but through love, has an undeniable similarity to Sufi doctrine.

The philosophical antecedent of Sufism, its origin, is the Spaniard Ibn 'Arabī (1165–1240), who taught the union with God through all His creations. The affinities of Ibn 'Arabī with Neoplatonism are only one aspect of his powerful thought. There is also an exalted eroticism, as expressed in his book of poems, *The Interpreter of Desire*. The union of opposites, whether in logic or in mystical experiences, has both a carnal and a cosmic aspect: the copulation of the feminine and masculine poles of the universe. Both poet and philosopher, Ibn 'Arabī, it is said, experienced a genuine epiphany in the form of a Persian woman whom he met in Mecca, and who showed him the way toward the union of human and divine love. Love opens the eyes to understanding, and the world of appearances that is this world is transformed into a world of apparitions; everything that we touch and see is divine. This synthesis of pantheism and monotheism, of belief in the divinity of the creation (the world) and belief in a creator God, was the basis, centuries later, of the thought of such great mystic poets of India as Tukaram and Kabīr.

Trying to Combine Two Traditions

A revealing fact: all these mystic poets wrote and sang in the vernacular languages, not in Sanskrit, Persian or Arabic. Tukaram (1598–1649), who wrote in Marathi, was a Hindu poet who was unafraid to refer to Islam in terms such as these: "The first among the great names is that of Allah. . . ." But he immediately affirms his pantheism: "You are in the One. . . . In [the vision of the One] there is no I or you. . . ." The emblematic figure of these movements is a lower-caste poet, a weaver from Benares, Kabīr (1440–1518). Kabīr was of Muslim origin. Unlike the majority of the Hindu poets, he professed a strict deism, no doubt in order to emphasize his attempt at uniting the two religions. He indiscriminately called that unique God by its Islam or Hindu name: Allah or Rāma (Vishnu). [Twentieth-century poet Rabindranath] Tagore translated Kabīr's poems because he saw in them the failed promise of what India could have become. For a modern historian, Kabīr was "a pioneer of devotional poetry in Hindi, using the vernacular language in order to popularize religious themes taken from both Hindu and Islamic traditions." This is, of course, true, but he was something more: a great poet. His vision was unitarian: "If God is in the mosque, to whom does this world belong? . . . If Rāma is in the image that you worship, who can know what happens outside? . . . Kabīr is the son of Allah and of Rāma. He is my *gurū*, he is my *pīr*." (*Gurū* is the Hindu word for a spiritual teacher, *pīr* is the Sufi term.) This powerful movement of popular devotion had no repercussions among the philosophers or the theologians, nor among the politicians of the two religions. It never turned into a new religion or a new politics, though the bhakti movement might have been the nucleus for the union of the two communities and the birth of a new India.

Islamic Rulers in a Mostly Hindu Land

by Waldemar Hansen

For most of its history India has been not a single kingdom or nation but rather a cultural zone tied together not only by religion, but also history, geography, and custom. The main political form in the region has in fact been the small kingdom, and until recent times these small kingdoms numbered in the hundreds. Even today this Indian zone is often referred to as South Asia, a term meant to encompass not only the modern democratic nation of India but also Sri Lanka, Nepal, Bhutan, and the Islamic nations of Pakistan and Bangladesh.

From approximately 1200 to 1757 large parts of India were ruled by Muslims. The most well-known of these, the Moguls, are the subject of the following selection. The Moguls were descended from central Asian warriors who claimed to be descendants of the great fourteenth-century conqueror Timur (or Tamerlane) and his predecessor, Genghis Khan. Their first Indian conquests came in 1526, and the Mogul dynasty continued to rule much of north India until 1757. Many historians claim than during the period of the so-called Great Moguls—Babur, Humayun, Akbar, Jahangir, Shah Jahan, and Aurangzeb—the language, food, music, painting, and architecture of modern Indian civiliza-

Waldemar Hansen, *The Peacock Throne: The Drama of Mogul India*. New York: Holt, Rinehart and Winston, 1972. Copyright © 1972 by Waldemar Hansen. Reproduced by permission of the publisher.

tion were created. Indeed the most well known of all Indian monuments, the Taj Mahal, was built by the Mogul emperor Shah Jahan as a tomb for his beloved wife, Mumtaz Mahal.

In the following selection New York City–based author and playwright Waldemar Hansen describes how the Moguls ruled over a mostly Hindu population caught up in timeless customs and religious rituals. He also suggests how, in turn, the Hindus influenced their new rulers.

Behind this House of Timur lay India—ageless, heterogeneous, overwhelming. Moslem strangers had brought a linear Mohammedan [Muslim] calendar in their saddles, hoping to challenge Hindu cyclical time. In that sense they represented something new, though nothing could really be new to India. From the standpoint of Hindu metaphysics she had even known the Moguls before, in staggeringly endless repetitions of the universe known as the day and night of Brahma. These Moguls were a part of Kali Yuga, the blackest age in the throw of cosmic dice. They would act out their tragedy, and India would watch them with compassion but without tears: she had witnessed too many tragedies.

India's Complex Past

Quite aside from Hindu metaphysics, the Moguls could only take possession for a historical moment. Like Egypt, India looked back on an incredibly long past in which she had always conquered her conquerors. Pastoral Aryans had come through those northwest passes to mingle over millennia with dark-skinned Dravidians, and only the complexities of Hinduism were left to reflect their absorption. Nobody even remembered the overrated intrusion of Alexander the Great. True, brilliant King Ashoka—a would-be Indian Constantine who converted to Buddhism—had briefly held universal sway long before the birth of Christ. But his dynasty disappeared, just as Buddhism itself had almost disappeared from India. In the endless welter of tuppenny [two-cent; i.e., insignificant] kings and limited empires that followed, nothing emerged but the fatal weakness of men whose narrow loyalties precluded grander unity. One final attempt to impose central imperial control had been made by the Guptas, who rose even as Rome was declining in the West. Then came invading Huns, and an interim period not unlike Europe's Dark Ages, with feudal states crystallizing into jigsaw pieces of power.

Now it was the turn of the Moguls. It was their India, impressive in variety and scope. A peregrine falcon soaring upward from some gloved Mogul wrist could have cast its rapacious eye over an empire which extended from Afghanistan to the Bay of Bengal, from the foot of the Himalayas to nervous southern kings of Bijapur and Golconda who lived in fear of annexation.

Skewered together, the fifteen provinces of Mogul Hindustan represented extreme ranges of climate and topography: deserts where water was more precious than gold, snow peaks, and saffron-dotted Kashmir valleys; there was the five-fingered river network of the Punjab, together with rice deltas of Bengal, alluvial tracts of [the rivers] Ganges and Jumna, black cotton soil of Nagpur plain, and wheatfields of a rich Narmada valley. In addition the Moguls had annexed an impressive slice (and intended to appropriate even more) of that mid-India which would later become their coffin—the Deccan. Enclosed by natural barriers of [the mountain chain] Western Ghats and northern hills, the Deccan was itself a varied enclave of lakes, tablelands which eons of erosion had sculpted into fantastic shapes, water-slashed ravines, and forests where the Asian lion was making its last stand.

Pullulating within these cells of empire, a hundred million subjects fell under Mogul hegemony—the Moslems, an ironic minority amid a mass of Hindus whose potential for rebellion against alien rule seemed for the moment neutralized by regional division, jealousy, and mistrust. It was all an ethnic beehive: heroic Rajput clans, fierce tribes swarming over Afghanistan plateaus, sturdy Jars, bearded Sikhs of the Punjab with combs gathering together the woman's-length hair which their religion forbade them to cut, and white-garbed Jains who considered all life so holy that they wore masks to avoid killing even a gnat by breathing. Islam alone bristled with sects and intrareligious frictions, to say nothing of the enormous complexities of a coexisting Hinduism with its rigid caste system and stubborn village autonomy. In addition, a heterogeneous assortment of adventurers—Turks, Persians, Tartars, Uzbeks, Circassians, and Georgians, even Africans and Europeans—made their way to the Mogul court.

Geographical, Human, and Religious Diversity

Though Humayun [the second Mogul emperor] had shown a predilection for Delhi, Agra still remained the chosen imperial capital. Both centers of empire were situated in north-central India on the Jumna River, which flowed southward until it finally conjoined with the holy Ganges at the stronghold of Allahabad. Aside from these royal twins, the realm vaunted other large cities—holy Hindu Banaras on the Ganges, Ajmer in the heart of Rajputana, Burhanpur in the Deccan, and Lahore, the great Punjab capital. The port of Surat (somewhat north of the Bombay which did not yet exist) was on the verge of becoming a busy target for foreign commerce and trade: English ambassadors seeking greater foothold for the newly formed East India Company, French gem merchants or doctors, Italian adventurers, and Portuguese intriguers sailing up the coast from their tiny enclave of Goa—droves of them would soon be arriving at Surat, making their way overland by bumpy ox caravan through certain key towns that led to Mogul Hindustan's heart.

But the great masses lived as they had always lived, in thatched and mud-baked huts of myriad villages which defined agrarian India. They grew rice and wheat, barley and millet and vegetables, tending their plots while water buffalo chewed cuds and wallowed in irrigation ditches. Goats, ducks, and skeletal cows wandered these rural precincts; every well had its cluster of bullock carts, swarthy men with burdens, women balancing water pots on their heads, and soulful children with great black eyes and black hair. Inevitable snake charmers and bear tamers heralded the approach to larger towns. Yet parts of the subcontinent also undulated in stretches of desolate wasteland. India then became a curious void, where people could only be invoked as part of a conjuring act.

Helping his descendants to rule such huge domains, Akbar had refined a practical realm based on familiar sources. No one could fail to recognize its affinity to old

Baghdad and Ispahan and the whole fairy-tale East: a quasi-Arab, quasi-Persian hierarchy had simply been adapted to an Indian setting. The emperor presided over his typically opulent Oriental court; he enjoyed an exclusive harem, where mysterious ladies were strictly veiled by jealous laws of purdah—the very word referred to screens of state behind which they viewed the spectacle of durbar [holding court]. Most of these women would be hidden from history in this candidly masculine Mogul world, though a few empresses and princesses asserted their vivid characters. Four in particular would become significant enough in Jahangir's and Shah Jahan's reigns to exert considerable influence on affairs of the realm.

Right hand to the emperor, the vizier or prime minister handled many important matters of state. There was, of course, no cabinet or parliament, though a few trusted officials might sometimes be consulted for advice. But the real pillars of empire in this bellicose Mogul autocracy were the nobility—soldier-grandees who did not inherit their rank but earned it, since every last man had to be ready for combat. Flowery imported titles of khan and khan khanan could be conferred on "holders of command" only by the Mogul emperor, who withdrew distinction whenever he liked. It was a dangerously arbitrary setup for such vital aristocrats; Mogul nobles constituted the very bulwark of bureaucracy, theoretically assigned to high civil and military appointments regardless of caste, creed, or race. . . .

The Challenges of Power

In any event, such a whirligig of Moslems and Hindus perpetually threatened to shatter into pieces through the accelerations of hatred, jealousy, and religious strife. Their centripetal bond was the powerful personality of the emperor himself—exactly what Akbar had in mind. It was all really a variation on knights in armor, an Oriental round table imported from the steppes of central Asia. Refined by India, the system intermittently worked in its own bizarre way; not a few nobles even proved loyal.

Provincial Mogul power balanced on a clever teeter-totter of military governors and nonmilitary tax collectors. Governors wielded power through armed forces, keeping contact with their village network by means of lesser functionaries; but only tax collectors could garner revenue through a retinue of appointed collections men, sending proceeds to the imperial treasury which then paid governor and collector alike. A spy fabric further assured royal control: news reporters sent weekly official reports to the capital, while there were secret agents whom no one knew.

Rounding out Mogul administration, Islamic justice prevailed. Every town had its Moslem chief of police and mullahs to apply Koranic law, though Hindu [pundits or brahmin religious advisers] were allowed to deal with transgressions in their own communities—a practical concession. Religion served additionally in matters of education: no public schools existed, and teaching reverted to mosque or Hindu temple.

Unable to leave wealth or property to their families, Mogul grandees lived in wild ostentation. Why invest private capital when accumulation might conceivably be appropriated by royal command? Such a system of escheat and obeisance made human volcanoes smolder. No wonder the nobility were forever revolting and the emperor obligingly forgiving them—a cheerful symbiosis. No barons extorted a Magna Charta [an agreement securing the rights of lesser nobles in England in 1215], no court went into voluntary exile if the emperor found himself dethroned, no mercantile class acted as buffer for the multitudes. Industry remained confined to state enterprises for the emperor, while art or literature found encouragement only by imperial prerogative. Europeans would soon be shocked at the sight of monarchic power carried to such excess. But then, the rules of any society are capricious on final examination.

If the Moguls had created this world of Eastern imperialism, what Atlas sustained it on his back? In agricultural India, Atlas could only be plural: he was the anonymous Hindu peasant. Amorphous and scorned by history, Hindustan's millions tilled the fields that fed an empire; assuredly much of the fruit of their hard work was appropriated (forcibly if need be) by Mogul revenue officers. In some districts, dark clouds obscuring the sky would be followed by hailstones as large as hens' eggs. The specter of famine hovered over masses already haunted by guinea worm, dysentery, cholera, plague, poxes, fevers, and venereal disease. Not that a Moslem court could ever be uncharitable—alms constituted one of Islam's five pillars—but sprays of silver and gold coins from imperial elephant processions could only afford momentary relief for rampant unimperial squalor.

Where exploitation is familiar, it endures for generations. Mogul land assessment was not so very different from Hindu methods rooted in thousands of years of *dharma* or sacred law—Akbar's revenue genius, Todar Mal, merely improved on a long-existing situation. There had always been a ruler who took from the Indian people; farmers had land tenure, it was their duty to pay. The trouble under Mogul rule was the amount of tax. Traditional Hindu assessment had been one-sixth of the land; but with these new conquerors; taxes increased from cupidity until (in spite of Akbar's or other emperors' good intentions) a third or even a half suffered appropriation, every dishonest Mogul official receiving his cut. Obviously, the system must ultimately break down from sheer greed; there was an end even to Hindu patience.

Hindu Influences on Their Rulers

Influential beyond measure, that Hindu majority contributed more to Mogul India than brow sweat. They and their ruling Moslems would and did interchange customs, clothing, ways, language. Members of the royal family already condescended to speak Hindustani in preference to Babur's Turkish tongue, though snobbish Persian had become the official court medium of exchange.

Still, religious differences were harder to reconcile, and Hinduism made orthodox Moslems uneasy. There was something ominous about an ageless theology which crammed everything into its maw—one godhead but endless gods, good and evil, light and dark, gentleness and violence. How could restless Moguls not be disturbed by "infidel" permissiveness? The holiest Hindus even blessed their conquerors with that same acceptance which over thousands of years had embraced everything mankind ever thought or felt or dreamt. Extremes of eroticism and repression, indulgence and abnegation found outlet in Hindu life. Weird sacrifice abounded: ecstatics pitched headlong beneath the wheels of Jagganaut on processional days, and women burned themselves alive in acts of suttee.

Yet Hinduism revered creation as much as destruction, fecundity as much as the ascetic. Hindus believed in Laxshmi, goddess of overflowing; reverence for life went to such lengths that bowls of milk were offered to temple cobras.

In its stubborn patterns of eternity, Hinduism passively rebuked those ticktock hours of Moslems and Christians. For Hindus, reincarnation and repetition transcended notions of once-only. Timeless Banaras, the Hindu Rome, afforded the same spectacle for the seventeenth century as it does today or did two thousand years ago. Multitudes of Hindus bathed in the holy Ganges by dawn, assumed the cross-legged lotus posture to greet a rising sun, and worshiped in tilting, half-submerged temples crowding the foreshore. Brahman priests sat under umbrellas by heaps of colored powders to be smeared on cheek or forehead. Cremation fires burned day and night while dogs lurked about the pyres; ashes of the dead were shoveled into a river already crowded with the living, so that posthumous union with the Hindu godhead might prevent endless rebirth in a world of suffering. Moguls saw the same penitents, wanderers, and stark-naked *sadhus* who can still be found along India's roads, together with costumes of dhoti and sari which have changed little over centuries. Indians were so profoundly conservative that they would "prefer an old Hell to a new Heaven!" It was all inordinately strange.

Of course, not everyone conformed or lived as a saint; Mogul India seethed with devils and rebels and crime. A random sampling of standard punishment seems more than revealing: captured thieves had their rights hands cut off, apprehended highwaymen lost both hands and feet, and robbers and apostates suf-

fered decapitation so that their heads could be im-
mured in edifying cement turrets. Even adulterers got
stoned to death, while fornicators could look forward
to a hundred lashes.

Such extreme penalties could only be designed to
suppress extreme disorder. Under Jahangir's new reign,
lone subjects without caravans were hardly safe on in-
secure public highways. Before long, the road from
Delhi to Agra would become infested with professional
assassins called thuggees. Devotees of Kali, the Hindu
goddess of death and destruction, thugs offered up
prayers for the success of their violent enterprises. Mur-
der represented the apotheosis of devotion and sacrifice, pickaxe and dagger being symbolic of the goddess's teeth and ribs. In remote areas, cutthroat bands
dominated whole provinces.

Everything added up to a sum of savage contrasts.
Without ever having known this East, [seventeenth-
century English poet] John Milton would soon encompass its dazzle and brutality in a single poetic epithet—
"barbaric pearl and gold."

A Devotional Poet on the Simplicity of Reaching God

by Kabir

During the period from approximately A.D. 1000 to 1500, many separate Hindu sects emerged which experts have referred to as bhakti sects. The word *bhakti* means "personal devotion to God," and these sects were part of the so-called absolutist school of Hinduism. This school, one of two major schools in Hinduism, teaches that there is an absolute godhead of which all other "gods," such as Shiva or Vishnu, are representations. The purpose of bhakti, like other absolutist rites, was to strive to achieve a clear intuitive understanding of the relationship between the godhead and the individual, generally through meditation or other personalized rites.

The following selection is from a poem by Kabir, a north Indian bhakti poet who lived from 1440 to 1518. Kabir, who some believe was born a Muslim or a low-caste Hindu, argues in this earthy translation that his believing brothers, whether Hindu or Muslim, should give up their rituals, asceticism, and learning in order to seek Ram, or God, who can truly be sought only by looking inward. He urges people to speak the name of Ram continually, a form of prayer within the bhakti tradition.

John Stratton Hawley and Mark Juergensmeyer, translators, "Kabir Granthavali," *Songs of the Saints of India.* New York: Oxford University Press, 1988. Copyright © 1988 by Oxford University Press, Inc. Reproduced by permission.

Go naked if you want,
Put on animal skins.
    What does it matter till you see the inward Ram?

If the union yogis seek
Came from roaming about in the buff,
    every deer in the forest would be saved.

If shaving your head
Spelled spiritual success,
    heaven would be filled with sheep.

And brother, if holding back your seed
Earned you a place in paradise,
    eunuchs would be the first to arrive.

Kabir says: Listen brother,
Without the name of Ram
    who has ever won the spirit's prize? . . .

Pundit, how can you be so dumb?
You're going to drown, along with all your kin,
    unless you start speaking of Ram.

Vedas, Puranas—why read them?
    It's like loading an ass with sandalwood!
Unless you catch on and learn how Ram's name goes,
    how will you reach the end of the road?

You slaughter living beings and call it religion:
    hey brother, what would irreligion be?
"Great Saint"—that's how you love to greet each other:
    Who then would you call a murderer?

Your mind is blind. You've no knowledge of yourselves.
    Tell me, brother, how can you teach anyone else?
Wisdom is a thing you sell for worldly gain,
    so there goes your human birth—in vain.

You say: "It's Narad's command."
   "It's what Vyas says to do."
   "Go and ask Sukdev, the sage."
Kabir says: you'd better go and lose yourself in Ram
   for without him, brother, you drown. . . .

Hey Qazi,
   what's that book you're preaching from?
And reading, reading—how many days?
   Still you haven't mastered one word.
Drunk with power, you want to grab me;
   then comes the circumcision.
      Brother, what can I say?—
If God had wanted to make me a Muslim,
   why didn't he make the incision?
You cut away the foreskin, and then you have a Muslim;
   so what about your women?
      What are they?
Women, so they say, are only half-formed men:
   I guess they must stay Hindus to the end.
Hindus, Muslims—where did they come from?
   Who got them started down this road?
Search inside, search your heart and look:
   Who made heaven come to be?
Fool,
   Throw away that book, and sing of Ram.
      What you're doing has nothing to do with him.
Kabir has caught hold of Ram for his refrain,
   And the Qazi?
      He spends his life in vain.

Sikhism Grows Out of the Hindu Tradition

by Hew McLeod

In the following selection Hew McLeod describes the spiritual origins and basic beliefs of Sikhism, aside from Buddhism the main independent religion to emerge out of Hindu India. A relatively new religion as far as major faiths go, Sikhism was founded by Guru Nanak in the early sixteenth century in a region of northwestern India known as the Punjab, an agricultural heartland which has been the common route of invaders into India and has served as a crossroad of peoples and ideas. McLeod suggests that Sikhism, far from being a new faith, was derived from a devotional, or bhakti, sect within Hinduism known as the Sant tradition. This tradition argued that each man could find the divine within himself. For Sikhs this process is most possible through a guru, or teacher.

From what was likely a spiritual community among hundreds of like communities, Sikhs emerged as an identifiable group in the sixteenth and seventeenth centuries. They developed a distinctive way of life involving, for men, never cutting their hair or beard (necessitating a turban), and wearing both a silver bracelet and a ceremonial dagger. They also acquired a reputation as fierce warriors, probably due to the need to de-

Hew McLeod, "Sikhism," *A Cultural History of India*, edited by A.L. Basham. London: Oxford University Press, 1975. Copyright © 1975 by Oxford University Press. All rights reserved. Reproduced by permission.

fend their community in the chaos of north India in the seventeenth and eighteenth centuries. In the twenty-first century the Sikhs remain an important minority in India, numbering over 20 million people, and Sikhs have accompanied Hindus to various expatriate communities in Britain, North America, and Australia. Hew McLeod was professor of history at the University of Otago in Dunedin, New Zealand.

Sikhism is generally held to derive from the teachings of the first Gurū, Nānak (1469–1539). In a sense this is true, for there can be no doubt that the doctrines which he taught survive within the community to this day. Moreover, there can be no doubt that a direct connection links the community of today with the group of disciples who first gathered around Nānak in the [Punjab] during the early years of the sixteenth century. In another sense, however, the claim is open to obvious objections. An analysis of the teachings of Nānak will demonstrate that the essential components of his thought were already current in the Indian society of his period. Nānak taught a doctrine of salvation through the divine Name. Others were already preaching this doctrine, and a comparison of their beliefs with those of the early Sikh community plainly shows that Nānak taught from within a tradition which had already developed a measure of definition.

Hindu Precursors

This was the *Nirguna Sampradāya*, or Sant tradition of northern India, a devotional school commonly regarded

as a part of the tradition of Vaishnava *bhakti* [devotion
to Krishna]. A connection between the Sants and the
Vaishnavas does indeed exist, but there are distinctive
features of Sant doctrine which distinguish it from its
Vaishnava antecedents. Most of these can be traced to its
other major source, Tantric Yoga. The most prominent
of the Sants prior to Nānak was Kabīr, and it is no doubt
due to the obvious similarities in their teachings that
Nānak has sometimes been represented as a disciple of
his predecessor. Although there is no evidence to support this supposition, the measure of doctrinal agreement which links them is beyond dispute.

This debt to the earlier Sant tradition must be acknowledged if there is to be any understanding of the
antecedents of Nānak's thought. It is, however, necessary to add that, as far as can be judged from surviving
Sant works, Nānak raised this inheritance to a level of
beauty and coherence attained by none of his predeces-
sors. From the quality of his [Punjabi] verses and the
clarity of the message expressed in them it is easy to appreciate why this particular man should have gathered
a following of sufficient strength to provide the nucleus of a continuing community. The evidence suggests that Nānak inherited a theory of salvation which
was at best incomplete and commonly naïve in its in-
sistence upon the adequacy of a simple repetition of a
particular divine name. Kabīr, master of the pithy epigram, was certainly not naïve, nor yet does he appear
to have been altogether clear and consistent. These are
qualities which one cannot always expect to find in a
mystic, and there can be no doubt that in Kabīr it was
the mystical strain which predominated. For Nānak
also salvation was to be found in mystical union with
God, but Nānak evidently differed in that he recog-

nized the need to explain in consistent terms the path to the ultimate experience. It is in the coherence and the compelling beauty of his explanation that Nānak's originality lies.

The thought of Nānak begins with two groups of basic assumptions. The first concerns the nature of God, who in an ultimate sense is unknowable. God, the One, is without form . . . , eternal . . . , and ineffable. . . . Considerable stress is thus laid upon divine transcendence, but this alone does not express Nānak's understanding of God. If it did there would be, for Nānak, no possibility of salvation. God is also gracious, concerned that men should possess the means of salvation and that these means should be abundantly evident to those who would diligently seek them. There is, Nānak insists, a purposeful revelation, visible to all who will but open their eyes and see. God is *sarab viāpak*, 'everywhere present', immanent in all creation, both within and without every man.

Both Hindus and Muslims Are Misled

The second group of assumptions concerns the nature of man. Men are by nature wilfully blind, shutting their eyes to the divine revelation which lies about them. They commonly appreciate the need for salvation, but characteristically seek it in ways which are worse than futile because they confirm and strengthen humanity's congenital blindness. The Hindu worships at the temple and the Muslim at the mosque. Misled by their religious leaders they mistakenly believe that external exercises of this kind will provide access to salvation. Instead they bind men more firmly to the transmigratory wheel of death and rebirth, to a perpetuation of suffering rather than to the attainment of bliss.

This, for Nānak, is *māyā* [illusion]. In Nānak's usage the term does not imply the ultimate unreality of the world itself, but rather the unreality of the values which it represents. The world's values are a delusion. If a man accepts them no amount of piety can save him. They must be rejected in favour of alternative values. Salvation can be obtained only through a recognition of the alternative, and through the faithful exercise of a discipline which demonstrably produces the desired result.

Nānak's teachings concerning the way of salvation are expressed in a number of key words which recur constantly in his works. God, being gracious, communicates his revelation in the form of the *śabad* (*śabda*, 'word') uttered by the *gurū* (the 'preceptor'). Any aspect of the created world which communicates a vision or glimpse of the nature of God or of his purpose is to be regarded as an expression of the *śabad*. The *gurū* who expresses, or draws attention to, this revelation is not, however, a human preceptor. It is the 'voice' of God mystically uttered within the human heart. Any means whereby spiritual perception is awakened can be regarded as the activity of the *gurū*.

Duly awakened by the *gurū*, the enlightened man looks around and within himself and there perceives the *hukam* (the divine 'order'). Like its English equivalent, the term *hukam* is used by Nānak in two senses, but it is the notion of harmony which is fundamental. Everywhere there can be perceived a divinely-bestowed harmony. Salvation consists in bringing oneself within this pattern of harmony.

This requires an explicit discipline, the practice of *nām simaran* or *nām japan*. The word *nām* ('name') signifies all that constitutes the nature and being of God; and the verb *simaranā* means 'to hold in remembrance'. The alternate verb *japanā* means, literally, 'to repeat', and for many of the Sants a simple, mechanical repetition of a chosen name of God (e.g. Rām) was believed to be a sufficient method. For Nānak much more is required. The pattern which he sets forth consists of a regular, disciplined meditation upon the *nām*. The essence of the *nām* is harmony and through this discipline the faithful devotee progressively unites himself with the divine harmony. In this manner he ascends to higher and yet higher levels of spiritual attainment, passing eventually into the condition of mystical bliss wherein all disharmony is ended and, in consequence, the round of transmigration is at last terminated. The proof of this is the experience itself. Only those who have attained it can know it.

For most people a reference to Sikhism will at once evoke an impression of beards, turbans, and martial valour. It rarely suggests doctrines of salvation through patient meditation upon the divine Name. Both, however, belong to Sikhism.

CHAPTER 3

Hinduism in the Recent Past and in Modern Times

Religions and Religious Movements

An Eighteenth-Century Englishwoman's Observations of Hindu Customs

by Eliza Fay

The following selection is from a collection of letters by Eliza Fay, an Englishwoman who married a man who planned a legal career in Calcutta in northeastern India. In the late 1700s when the Fays made their way to Calcutta, the city was fast becoming the main British city in India; indeed in later years it was called the second capital of the British Empire (after London).

Although British traders had lived in India since the early 1600s, it was only from 1757 that Britain could truly be said to maintain large colonial possessions there. In that year, thanks to their participation in a series of wars involving various Indian kings as well as the French, Britain had been granted possession of Bengal, a rich province where Calcutta was located. Over the years British territory expanded until the small European kingdom became the dominant power in India, a situation which ended only with Indian independence in 1947.

Eliza Fay, then, was among the earliest English observers of Indian customs. Although many English people took pains to understand Hindu history and reli-

Eliza Fay, *Original Letters from India (1779–1815)*. London: Hogarth Press, 1986.

gious practice, Fay was more typical of the ordinary English visitors and residents who found Hindu customs bewildering and sometimes shocking. Here she comments on such matters as caste and the status of women.

I now propose, having full leisure to give you some account of the East Indian customs and ceremonies, such as I have been able to collect, but it must be considered as a mere sketch, to point your further researches. And first for that horrible custom of widows burning themselves with the dead bodies of their husbands; the fact is indubitable, but I have never had an opportunity of witnessing the various incidental ceremonies, nor have I ever seen any European who had been present at them. I cannot suppose that the usage originated in the superior tenderness, and ardent attachment of Indian wives towards their spouses, since the same tenderness and ardour would doubtless extend to his offspring and prevent them from exposing the innocent survivors to the miseries attendant on an orphan state, and they would see clearly that to live and cherish these pledges of affection would be the most rational and natural way of shewing their regard for both husband and children. I apprehend that as personal fondness can have no part here at all, since all matches are made between the parents of the parties who are betrothed to each other at too early a period for choice to be consulted, this practice is entirely a political scheme intended to insure the care and good offices of wives to their husbands, who have not failed in most countries to invent a sufficient number of rules to render the weaker sex totally subservient to their authority. I cannot avoid smiling when

I hear gentlemen bring forward the conduct of the Hindoo women, as a test of superior character, since I am well aware that so much are we the slaves of habit *every where* that were it necessary for a woman's reputation to burn herself in England, many a one who has *accepted* a husband merely for the sake of an establishment, who has lived with him without affection; perhaps thwarted his views, dissipated his fortune and rendered his life uncomfortable to its close, would yet mount the funeral pile with all imaginable decency and die with heroic fortitude. The most specious sacrifices are not always the greatest, she who wages war with a naturally petulant temper, who practises a rigid self-denial, endures without complaining the unkindness, infidelity, extravagance, meanness or scorns, of the man to whom she has given a tender and confiding heart, and for whose happiness and well being in life all the powers of her mind are engaged;—is ten times more of a heroine than the slave of bigotry and superstition, who affects to scorn the life demanded of her by the laws of her country or at least that country's custom; and many such we have in England, and I doubt not in India likewise: so indeed we ought, have we not a religion infinitely more pure than that of India? The Hindoos, or gentoos are divided into four castes or tribes called the Brahmin, the Khutree, the Buesho, and the Shodor; [Brahmin, Kshatriya, Vaisya, and Shudra] their rank in the land, declines gradually to the last named, and if any of them commit an offence which deprives them of the privileges that belong to their respective castes, they become Parias, [pariahs, or outcasts] which may therefore be called a filthy tribe formed as it were of the refuse of the rest. Those are indeed considered the very dregs of the people, and supply all the lowest offices of human life. They all profess what is called the religion of Brahma, from the caste which bears his name all the priests are chosen, who are treated in every respect with distinguished honour and reverence. Their religious Code is contained in a book called the Veda, which only the Brahmins are allowed to read; it is written in a dead language called the Sanscrit. They worship three Deities, Brahma, the creator, Vistnoo the preserver, and Sheevah the destroyer. But they profess to believe them only the representations or types of the great spirit Brahma (the Supreme God) whom they also call the spirit of wisdom, and the principle of Truth: none but Hindoos are allowed to enter temples, but I am told the Idols worshipped there are of the very ugliest forms that imagination can conceive; and to whom [poet Alexander] Pope's description of the heathen deities may, in other respects, be strictly applied.

Gods changeful, partial, passionate unjust.
Whose attributes *are* rage, revenge, or lust.

I lament to add to such wretched objects as these, numbers of the deluded natives are devoted in the strongest and most absolute manner possible. A certain sect named Pundarams live in continual beggary; extreme hunger alone induces them to ask for food, which when granted, they only take just what will preserve life, and spend all their days in singing songs in praise of Sheevah; another sect add a tabor, and hollow brass rings about their ancles to increase the noise with which they extol *their* deity. I consider both these as a species of monks but believe the holy fathers fall far short of the Jogees and Seniase [yogis and sanayasis, or holy men] of India, in their religious austerities. These not only endure all possible privations with apparent indifference, but invent for themselves various kinds of tortures which they carry to an astonishing length; such as keeping their hands clenched till the nails grow into them,—standing on one foot for days and even weeks together—and hiring people to support their hands in a perpendicular position.

Unusual Rituals and Practices

Their expiatory punishments are some of them dreadful. I myself saw a man running in the streets with a piece of iron thrust through his tongue which was bleeding profusely. On the Churruk Poojah (swinging feast) hundreds I have heard, are suspended at an amazing height by means of hooks, firmly fixed in the flesh of the back, to which sometimes a cloth is added round the body to afford the miserable victim a chance of escape, should the hook give way. I, by accident, (for voluntarily nothing should have tempted me to witness such a spectacle) saw one of these wretches, who was whirling round with surprizing rapidity, and at that distance scarcely appeared to retain the semblance of a human form. They firmly expect by this infliction to obtain pardon of all their offences, and should death be the consequence, they go straight to heaven—thus changing the horrid state of privation and misery in which they exist here, for one of bliss: if such be their real persuasion, who can condemn the result.

Indeed under other circumstances it is found that, notwithstanding their apparent gentleness and timidity, the Hindoos will meet death with intrepid firmness—they are also invincibly obstinate, and will *die* rather than concede a point: of this a very painful instance has lately occurred.—A Hindoo beggar of the

Brahmin caste went to the house of a very rich man, but of an inferior tribe, requesting alms; he was either rejected, or considered himself inadequately relieved, and refused to quit the place. As his lying before the door and thus obstructing the passage was unpleasant, one of the servants first intreated, then insisted on his retiring, and in speaking pushed him gently away; he chose to call this push a blow, and cried aloud for redress, declaring that he would never stir from the spot till he had obtained justice against the man: who now endeavoured to sooth him but in vain; like a true Hindoo he sat down, and never moved again, but thirty-eight hours afterwards expired, demanding justice with his latest breath; being well aware that in the event of this, the master would have an enormous fine to pay, which accordingly happened. I am assured that such evidences of the surprizing indifference to life, the inflexible stubbornness, and vindictive dispositions of these people are by no means rare; it seems extraordinary though, that sentiments and feelings apparently so contrary to each other should operate on the same minds; seeing them so quiet and supine, so (if it may be so expressed) only half alive, as they generally shew themselves, one is prepared for their sinking, without an effort to avert any impending danger; but that they should at the same time nourish so violent and active a passion as revenge, and brave even death so intrepidly as they often do in pursuit of it, is very singular:— but enough of these silly enthusiasts.

A Hindoo Wedding

I had lately the opportunity of witnessing the marriage procession of a rich Hindoo. The bride (as I was told) sat in the same palanquin with the bridegroom, which was splendidly ornamented;—they were accompanied by all the relations on both sides, dressed in the most superb manner;—some on horse back, some in palanquins, and several on elephants;—bands of dancing girls and musicians I understood preceded them;—and in the evening there were fireworks at the bride's father's house and the appearance of much feasting &c. but no Europeans were present. This wedding was of a nature by no means uncommon here; a rich man had an only daughter, and he bargained to dispose of her, or rather to take for her a husband out of a poor man's family, but of his own *Caste:* for this is indispensable. In this case the bridegroom is brought home to his father-in-law's house and becomes a member of the family; so that although the law prohibits a man from giving a dowry with his daughter, yet you see he does it in effect, since he gives a house to a man who wants one; gives in fact, a fortune but saddled with an encumbrance;—perhaps in a few years the old man may die, and the young one having fulfilled the wishes of his parents, and provided for his own wants, may employ some of his female relations to look round among the poorer families of his caste for a pretty girl, whom he will take as a second wife, tho' the first always retains the pre-eminence, and governs the house; nor can the husband devote more of his time to one than the other,—the law compelling him to live with them alternately, you may be sure the account is strictly kept. My Banian [shopkeeper] Dattaram Chuckerbutty has been married between twenty and thirty years, without taking a second lady, and he boasts of being much happier with his old wife (as he calls her) than the generality of his friends are amidst the charms of variety. For my own part, I have not a doubt but he is in the right.

The Hindoo ladies are never seen abroad; when they go out their carriages are closely covered with curtains, so that one has little chance of satisfying curiosity. I once saw two apparently very beautiful women: they use so much art however, as renders it difficult to judge what claim they *really* have to that appellation—Their whole time is taken up in decorating their persons:— the hair—eye-lids—eye-brows—teeth—hands and nails, all undergo certain processes to render them more completely fascinating; nor can one seriously blame their having recourse to these, or the like artifices—the motive being to secure the affections of a husband, or to counteract the plans of a rival.

Funeral Customs

The Hindoos who can afford to purchase wood for a funeral pile, burn their dead; one cannot go on the river without seeing numbers of these exhibitions, especially at night, and most disgusting spectacles they are. I will not enlarge on the subject. This mode however is far superior to that of throwing them into the river as practised by the poor; where they offend more senses than one. I have been frequently obliged to return precipitately from a walk along the river side, by the noisome exhalations which arose from these wretched objects.

Some of the Hindoo customs respecting the sick are really shocking—When a person is given over by the Brahmins, (who are physicians as well as priests) the relations immediately carry him, if within a reasonable distance, to the banks of the Ganges, where he is smeared with the mud, quantities of which I am told are thrust into his mouth, nose, and ears. This treatment soon reduces him to a dying state; nor is it desirable that he should recover, since he must in that case lose caste; for it is an established rule, that whoever removes from the spot where the sacred rites have been performed, becomes an outcast. Dr. Jackson was once fortunate enough to be called in to attend the wife of a Hindoo Rajah [prince] whom they were on the point of taking to the river when he arrived—he assured the Rajah that he perceived no dangerous symptoms and would answer for her doing well.—Luckily the tremendous ceremonies had not commenced: The event justified our good Doctor's predictions—the lady is still living and his success in this instance, has led to several others, highly gratifying to the best feelings of humanity and certainly beneficial to his fortune.

Hindu Responses to British Rule

by Norvin Hein

Great Britain ruled India, either directly or along with certain local kings known as maharajahs, from 1757 until 1947. Inevitably these new foreign rulers had an impact on Indian culture in general and on certain Hindu practices in particular. Among the most visible legacies of British rule is the fact that even today English is the common language of a subcontinent where some seventeen other major languages are spoken.

In the following selection scholar Norvin Hein describes the impact that British rule had on Hinduism. He emphasizes that one of the important challenges to Hinduism, a religion not overly concerned with material welfare or improving life on earth, was simply the arrival of the modern world. Economic practices, Western-style education, and industrial technology all had their impact on the religion. He also examines reactions to these changes in the forms of Hindu modernist, fundamentalist, and nationalist movements. These movements not only helped Hindus reconcile their religious beliefs with the modern world, they also challenged, in some instances, such long-standing customs as the caste system. Moreover they played a role in India's independence movement as part of a larger overall attempt to carve out a new sense of Indian identity and nationhood. The author suggests as well that this legacy survives in Hindu fundamentalist movements. Norvin Hein is professor emeritus of religion at Yale University.

The two centuries of British rule [from 1757 to 1947] . . . were much more disturbing to the Hindus' outlook than were the five preceding centuries of Muslim control, despite the latter's aggressive attitude toward Hinduism. There were two reasons for India's stronger reaction to the British presence. First, the British, unlike the Muslims, brought to India powerful new economic institutions. The development of Western shipping on the Indian coast drew India into a worldwide commercial network for the large-scale exchange of goods, and soon Calcutta, Bombay, Madras, and inland cities as well became huge trading centers.

This development brought with it a great increase in the proportion of the population engaged in trade and making a living outside the economic system of India's tightly knit villages. Of all caste Hindus, the merchants had always been the most free to adopt whatever forms of religion they wished, and now much larger classes of people in the new commercial centers became immune to economic pressures toward conformity. Family and caste assemblies could still bring heavy pressure on their individual members, but the termination of livelihood—the threat that had kept members of the village communities in line—could no longer be used effectively. When the Industrial Revolution reached India and factories became a major source of livelihood in the towns, millions of Hindus became free to follow radical religious leaders of their own personal choice.

The second reason for the Indians' strong reaction to British culture was the activity of the British government in promoting education. Although the network of educational institutions at first supported by the British government was minimal by present-day standards, it far exceeded the public education offered by previous Hindu and Muslim rulers. Early in the nineteenth century, some schools began to teach Western learning as well as traditional Indian subjects: as early as 1817 the Hindu College was established in Calcutta to instruct young men in the English language and literature, and Christian missionaries soon opened similar schools and colleges.

Education in English

The Hindus' response was positive. In 1835 a momentous decision was made to conduct government-supported education mainly in English and to make the Western arts and sciences a principal part of the curriculum. In the same period European printing presses, set up in India in unprecedented numbers, made the literature of European culture easily available to the many who could read English. Thus the meeting between East and West that had previously been mainly physical began to acquire a deeper dimension.

In order to appreciate the collision of ideas that occurred, we need to examine the Hinduism prevailing in about 1800 and the shocking contrasts with which it was confronted. In the popular cults, many of the Hindu practices at the beginning of the nineteenth century concentrated on finding protection against the dangers of the natural world. On the doctrinal level, the central Hindu ideas had the function of supporting the caste system. Belief in karma and rebirth rationalized the assignment of hereditary work and unequal distribution of opportunities and honors and justified the subjection of women in general and harsh treatment of widows in particular. The deprivations that old Hinduism imposed on many were made tolerable by teaching the evil of material desires, by offering loftier satisfactions in transcendent realms, and by denying the significance—or even the very reality—of the whole physical world. Hinduism provided no rationale for attempting to change the world. The way to happiness lay in a personal liberation from the world, not in trying to transform it into a place of freedom and bliss. Even the Bhagavadgita, despite its recognition of the need to support social institutions, did not advise dwelling long in this world, either physically or spiritually. . . .

It was the soul, not the world, that was deemed capable of salvation. The corporate progress of a people did not fall within the terms of Hindu thought. Even the idea of nation had no adequate expression in the terminology of Indian languages.

The British brought to India in the early nineteenth century a social optimism unusual even in Western history. An advancing medical science offered the possibility of freedom from disease, and the Industrial Revolution held out the possibility of freedom from poverty. Injustices could be identified and righted, and the world could be perfected. In this Western dream of social progress, nations figured as prominently as did individuals. From its base in biblical thinking, the Western mind conceived of the nation as a fundamental unit of moral responsibility and as a soteriological community. The British brought with them a pride and hope in their nation that the Hindus at first perceived as a refreshing model of virtue.

The Europeans of that time were able not only to proclaim an eloquent faith in the world's regeneration but also to take actions toward that end with impressive results. The power of Western learning was as obvious to Hindu observers as the power of the new steamboats that could transport their huge cargoes upstream on Indian rivers. Vaccination was clearly more effective for its purpose than offerings to the smallpox goddess. Young Hindus did not take long to decide that they wanted to learn the Western knowledge and to participate in its power.

This clear decision among the early generations of Western-educated Indians began very soon to produce new movements within Hinduism. Between 1800 and 1947 there were few Hindu champions of innovation who were not also reformers of religion. The first of the Hindu movements that reflect the Western impact is the Brahmo Samaj, founded in 1828 by a Bengali brahman named Ram Mohan Roy (1772–1833).

The Brahmo Samaj (Society of Believers in Brahman)

For generations Ram Mohan Roy's family had served Muslim rulers. He was sent as a boy to Muslim schools, where he learned Persian and Arabic and absorbed Muslim attitudes, including hostility toward the British. However, in 1803 he went into the revenue service of the East India Company, and under the guidance of a friendly British official Ram Mohan perfected his knowledge of English. Becoming acquainted with English literature and Western thought, he reversed his original negative opinion of Western culture and became a supporter of a temporary British rule over India and an advocate of Western education.

In 1814 Ram Mohan Roy retired from government service to promote his ideas regarding religion and morality. He denounced polytheism, idolatry, and certain Hindu social practices he deemed harmful to society. He decried the Hindus' neglect of women's education and their treatment of widows, and he supported, in 1829, the British government's decision to abolish by law the practice of burning widows alive at the time of their husbands' cremation. He promoted the founding of colleges and schools to teach Western literature and science.

Western Influences

Early in his retirement Ram Mohan studied the Bible under the guidance of Christian missionaries. He developed a lasting admiration for the moral precepts and example of Jesus but was unable to accept the Christian belief in Jesus' divinity or in the atoning value of his death. Then Ram Mohan examined the Upanishads and Vedanta sutras [Hindu scriptures] and concluded that they taught a simple monotheism entirely free of polytheism and idolatry. He rested his monotheistic belief, therefore, on the Upanishads, which are counted as part of the authoritative vedic literature, and argued for the recognition of his beliefs as vedic and orthodox teaching.

In 1828 Ram Mohan founded the Brahmo Samaj, a religious association that met weekly thereafter for a congregational style of worship that is quite unusual in Hinduism. It included prayers, hymns, and sermons expounding such scriptures as the Kena, Isa, Mundaka, and Katha Upanishads.

The members who were gathered into the new society were usually persons of high social position and good education. After Ram Mohan's death the Brahmo Samaj was guided by new leaders whose demands for reform became increasingly incompatible with orthodox Hinduism.

Under the leadership of Debendranath Tagore (1817–1905), the Brahmo Samaj studied the Vedas more thoroughly and dropped its claim to orthodoxy. Taking reason and conscience rather than the Vedas as the final authority in religion, the Brahmo Samaj taught thereafter that scriptures were to be regarded as valid only when their message was confirmed by a light within the heart. In the society's earlier period its members had been urged only to make no claim to superior dignity by reason of their high caste, but now they were asked to repudiate their caste identities entirely. The society pressed for laws against child marriage, attacked polygamy, and for the old samskara rituals devised replacements from which all references to the many gods were eliminated. Throughout the nineteenth century the Brahmo Samaj kept the Hindu upper classes in an uproar of argument for and against their daring demands.

Sharp differences of opinion divided and weakened the group in the latter part of the century, and today the Brahmo Samaj has only a few thousand members. The movement's theological ideas have not become dominant in modern Hinduism, but the members of the Brahmo Samaj won their social battles, so substantially altering public opinion, that by 1900 it was no longer necessary for Hindus to surrender membership in family and caste when they undertook to attack the inequities and extravagances of traditional Hinduism.

The Arya Samaj (Aryan Society)

About the time that the reformist commotion of the Brahmo Samaj was at its height in Bengal, [Swami] Dayananda Sarasvati (1824–1883) launched a very different campaign for change in northwestern India. ([Swami] is a title of respect given to a religious teacher.) Born to a devout Saiva [Shiva-worshipping] family in Gujarat, Dayananda at an early age rejected the worship of [Shiva]. Becoming an ascetic (sannyasi) at twenty-one, he wandered for some years in search of a satisfactory faith. At last in Mathura he found his guru in a fiery and eccentric teacher named Virajananda, who allowed his disciples to study nothing but Sanskrit grammar and a few of the oldest vedic scriptures. Virajananda loathed the puranas [holy stories] and all the popular gods of Hinduism. In 1863 Dayananda began his own campaigns against polytheism and idolatry. Lecturing in Sanskrit before priestly audiences, he attacked pujas [devotional offerings] and pilgrimages, denied the divinity of Rama and [Krishna] and asserted that the brahmans had no hereditary rights.

A Purified Hinduism

In 1874 Dayananda began to address more popular groups in Hindi with much success and wrote in Hindi his principal book, *The Light of Truth*. The following year he founded the Arya Samaj. It spread quickly throughout the Hindi-speaking areas, making the following major proclamations:

a) India is called on to resume its allegiance to the oldest religious literature of the land. The Vedas alone—by which Dayananda meant the four original collections, or samhitas—are the Word of God. The Brahmanas and Upanishads are authoritative only when they are in full agreement with the samhitas. Dayananda had no use whatsoever for the puranas and the smritis [scriptural traditions]—not even for the Bhagavadgita.

b) Since the word jati [caste] is not found in the Vedas, hereditary occupational castes have no place in true Hindu religion. But because the names of the four varnas [social classes] are found in the Vedas, the terms brahman, ksatriya, vaisya, and sudra may be used to refer to flexible classes to which Aryans may belong, not according to birth, but according to their level of ability. Anyone may study the Vedas. Today the Arya Samaj promotes the education of women, permits widows to remarry, allows intercaste dining and even intercaste marriage, and denounces child marriage and polygamy.

c) The Vedas are the source of all truth, scientific as well as religious. Using an unusual method of translation, Arya Samaj scholars have found in the Vedas proof that the sages who recorded them worshiped only one God, of personal nature, and that they were already acquainted millions of years ago with such supposedly modern inventions as the steam engine, telegraph, and airplane. According to the Arya Samaj, Indians who were taking up the study of Western science were merely recovering an Indian knowledge that had been lost.

d) The Vedas record the original religion of humanity and are the ultimate source of whatever truths non-Hindu faiths may still retain in a corrupted form. *The Light of Truth* gives Hinduism the central place in the historical development of the world's religions. The book vilifies Islam,

Christianity, and those forms of Hinduism that Dayananda detested, and it begins an important modern tendency toward the glorification of Hinduism in superlative terms.

As a movement, the Arya Samaj has been bitterly hostile to foreign cultural influences in India. Dayananda combated the resurgent Muslim movements of the mid-nineteenth century and opposed the missionary activities of Christians. For the first fifty years of its existence, the society continued to gather into its fellowship many reform-minded, middle-class Hindus. No longer seen as a shockingly radical organization, the Arya Samaj exists quietly today as a stable religious group with about half a million members. Though the Arya Samaj does not participate as an organization in politics, it has revived a long-lost understanding that civic concerns are religious concerns. Many of its members are important public figures.

Hindu Religious Nationalism

Swami Dayananda's controlled resentment of Western cultural influence in India was a light squall preceding a hurricane. In the late nineteenth century the sons of upper-class Indian families began to graduate from Indian universities with a new ambivalence of feeling toward Western culture. Western studies, like cut flowers transplanted from another garden, had failed to root successfully in Indian soil. Even those students who acquired a deep knowledge of the West were often offended by the aloofness of the Europeans in India who did not grant them the dignity of full acceptance in a world culture.

About this time, the research of European scholars

into India's forgotten past uncovered records of a happier and greater India of pre-Islamic times, in which enlightened Hindu rulers had patronized brilliant systems of thought and great works of literature and art. Hindu religious leaders now called on the young men of India to identify themselves with that brighter ancient heritage, and beginning about 1890 a passionate nationalism with religious overtones began to grow in the minds of many literate young Hindus. They viewed the West as a crass and worldly civilization, advanced only in the natural sciences, and in contrast, they saw the East as a spiritual culture destined to teach the world the art of lofty living. The rule of foreigners came to be regarded as a moral outrage. All the emotional devices of the Way of Devotion were brought into the service of a new object of devotion, the Indian nation itself, and the liberation of India became the goal of final blessedness for this half-religious nationalism.

India was sometimes conceived as a divine Mother in the form of the goddess Kali. Beginning in 1905 secret societies were organized, especially in Bengal, for violent revolutionary action. At altars of Kali, on which revolvers had been heaped, recruits vowed to bring bloody offerings to the Mother. A training manual entitled *Bhavani Mandir* (The temple of Kali) assured future assassins that their acts would bring the world to the light of Hinduism. Between 1908 and 1917 more than a hundred officials of the British government were killed or wounded by members of such societies. But nationalists in the Hindi-speaking areas, less accustomed than the Bengalis to making blood offerings to Kali, cultivated a reverence for a milder figure called Bharat Mata (Mother India).

The first great political leader of Hindu ultranationalism was Bal Gangadhar Tilak (1856–1920), a brahman from western India. In honor of the god Ganesha, the elephant-headed son of Shiva, Tilak devised a new festival as an occasion for carrying anti-British songs and dramas to the people, and he taught the Bhagavadgita with emphasis on such militant lines as "Fight, O son of Bharata!" (2.18). Chauvinistic nationalism reached its peak in the first two decades of the twentieth century, but it has continued to have strong spokesmen. A protégé of Tilak named V.C. Savarkar (1883–1966) organized the Hindu Mahasabha, a cultural society for the promotion of Hindu nationalism. The Hindu Mahasabha created as an auxiliary a young men's uniformed action group called the Rashtriya Svayamsevak Sangha, popularly known as the R.S.S. To extend its influence in Indian legislatures, the R.S.S. in 1951 established a political party called the Bharatiya Jan Sangh (Indian People's Party). The basic premise of these groups is that India must be preserved by insisting on a fivefold unity: one land, one race, one religion, one culture, and one language. They believe that Pakistan and Bangladesh must be reunited with India and with Hinduism, and that all Muslim, British, and other foreign influences in India must be eliminated.

Mahatma Gandhi's Hinduism

by Percival Spear

Probably the most identifiable Hindu leader of recent times is Mohandas K. Gandhi, a figure celebrated in India and internationally due to his advocacy of nonviolence and universal human rights. Indeed, Gandhi has achieved such renown that he is known as Mahatma, or Great Soul, and he enjoys the status of a holy man among most Hindus. In the following selection, historian Percival Spear describes Gandhi's contributions to India's independence movement from Great Britain.

Gandhi proved to be very liberal with regard to relations among different religions and to caste restrictions. He had a particular soft spot for untouchables, among the most oppressed people in India. He dubbed them "harijans," or children of god. He rooted his beliefs in ancient Hindu teachings such as those in the Vedas. He also, as Spear indicates, led by being an example of a man who favored tolerance and simplicity, and he learned how to use his public image effectively to appeal to a diverse, poor, and often illiterate population. While other leaders involved themselves in negotiations and deal making with the British, Gandhi turned the drive for Indian independence into a mass movement. Unfortunately his version of Hinduism proved to

Percival Spear, "Mahatma," *A History of India*. Vol. 2. Middlesex, England: Penguin Books, 1965. Copyright © 1965 by Percival Spear. Reproduced by permission of the publisher.

be too tolerant for some, and he was assassinated by a group of fundamentalist Hindus in January 1948, only a few months after India achieved its independence. Percival Spear worked for the British colonial government in India before taking up a lectureship in South Asian history at the University of Cambridge.

Mahatma Gandhi . . . was born at Porbandar, a small state in Kathiawar, in 1869. His father was the hereditary *diwan* or prime minister and his family belonged to the *vaish* or merchant caste. This group in the Kathiawar peninsula was closely connected with the sect of the Jains, with whom *ahimsa* or non-violence was a cardinal principle. From the start, therefore, Gandhi was brought up against a background of affairs, though on a small scale, and of pacifism, though this was not a prominent feature of Hinduism as a whole. He was also dissociated from the priestly Brahmin hierarchy. His early life is described vividly and meticulously in his *Story of My Experiments with Truth.* He was married as a boy to a child-wife and sent as a youth to London where he qualified as a barrister-at-law. This venture caused a split in his caste on his return, many of the members considering that he had broken caste by his journey overseas. The London period was the first turning-point in his life. He remained a vegetarian under difficulties and began his dietetic experiments. He came into touch with liberal and Christian ideas and the then novel teachings of [Russian novelist Leo] Tolstoy. He had his first experiences of racialism and British aloofness. On return he practised law in India for a time and then proceeded to South Africa where the existence of an Indian community formed by the immigration of indentured labour provided openings for a young man willing to live abroad. Gandhi stayed in South Africa until he was nearly forty-six. It was the second formative period in his life. Here he developed his ideas from a mixture of Christian, Hindu, and humanitarian sources. He raised a family and used them as specimens for his dietetic experiments, he assumed the leadership of the Indian community and used them as a laboratory for experiments in non-violence. He became convinced that western civilization was corrupt and violence a canker of society. He kept in touch with India through his friendship with [Gopal Krishna] Gokhale [a leader of India's independence movement] whom he regarded as his *guru* or teacher and whose Servants of India Society of political and social missionaries he planned to join on his return. He expressed his ideas in a little book written at white heat on board ship between Africa and India in 1909 called *Hind Swaraj* [*India Awake*].

This was the man, slight, bespectacled, and deprecating in manner, apparently the reverse of a man of action, who stirred the Indian masses to the depths, who swept the rugged veteran [Indian nationalist leader Bal Gangadhar] Tilak into oblivion, and who controlled the national movement for nearly twenty-eight years. A further experience awaited him in the first few years after his return to India. The poverty of the masses, whether the *kisans* [low-caste laborers] on the indigo estates of Bihar, or in his own Gujarat, burnt into his soul. A mass leader, he considered, must identify himself with those he aspired to lead; and he must not only lead but raise them. Motives of both compassion and policy led him in 1921 to discard his dapper European clothes, not for the *swami's* saffron robe, but for the peasant's homespun cotton *dhoti* [loincloth] and shawl. It was this gesture which finally won the hearts of the people and marked him in their eyes as a great soul.

Gandhi's Open-Minded Hinduism

Gandhi's mystique consisted of a union of original ideas (or an original pattern of known ideas) with a remarkable flair for tactics and an uncanny insight into the mass or peasant mind. He considered himself a Hindu but he was by no means an orthodox one. He took certain ideas, expanded them, and gradually wove them into a system which was ethical and spiritual as well as practical and political. He came to believe that his ideas formed a universal ethic, as applicable to [Nazi leader Adolf] Hitler and [Russian Communist leader Joseph] Stalin as to Hindus. He believed in the rights of man which led him at once into collision, not only with the British and South Africans, but with Hindu caste distinctions and their attitude to the 'Untouchables'. He removed his own sacred thread when he found that the fourth (Sudra) caste, was not allowed to wear it; and he christened the untouchables or outcasts *Harijans* or Sons of God. He welcomed them into his *ashram* [religious retreat and school] and found various ways of emphasizing their equality with others. He put humanity before caste rule and on an occasion ordered the mercy killing of a stricken sacred calf. These things did not endear him to the orthodox and it was a Brahmin who eventually struck him down. On this basis of fearless communal self-criticism he equally fearlessly claimed equal political rights for his countrymen.

Nonviolence and the Struggle for Truth

At the heart of his ideas lay the doctrine of *ahimsa* or non-violence. Violence was the expression of unreason and hate, the antithesis of love, and love was the essence of the spirit which permeates the universe. Therefore the opponent must be met by reason and entreaty; if he insisted on violence this must be borne cheerfully as a form of self-purification. Accepted suffering, in Gandhi's view, had healing and converting qualities. The opponent, unmoved by reason, would be won by cheerful suffering in a good cause. Along with *ahimsa* went severe self-discipline which included vows and fasts of purification and penance. Non-violence was the most spectacular side of Gandhi's thought, but its centre was the concept of *satya* or truth. *Ahimsa* was only one expression or outworking as it were of *satya* which was the pervasive spirit of man's life and the object of all his endeavours. It can perhaps be compared with the Platonic idea of justice as the art of right living. Truth was what man had to pursue with all his strength, self-discipline, his personal equipment, and non-violence or *ahimsa* his method of proceeding. Those who dedicated their lives to this pursuit were *satyagrahis* or truth-fighters. This was the name chosen for his specially trained followers or *élite*. Truth found expression in many ways. Within, it was the old Vedantic ideal of self-realization, which Gandhi dramatized as listening to the Inner Voice, as Socrates had his 'demon'; in politics it was freedom from foreign domination, the welding of a united nation; in Hindu society it was the breaking down of barriers raised by caste and age-old custom. In society at large it was living as close to nature as possible. Gandhi envisaged a peasant society of self-supporting workers, with simplicity as its ideal and purity as its hall-mark; the state would be a loose federation of village republics. He rejected the mechanics of the west along with its glitter and preached the necessity of hand spinning and weaving while cheerfully receiving the contributions of Indian industrialists.

Gandhi's Popular Appeal

Gandhi united various elements of Hinduism and other creeds in a highly original way. He dramatized his ideas by a constant stream of articles, speeches, and declarations, and above all by his own example. Gandhi, in the peasant's loin-cloth and shawl, sitting at the spinning wheel, writing notes on his weekly day of silence, sitting lost in contemplation or lying exhausted during a fast, were all ways of getting his image across to a largely illiterate population. They were not Brahminic, priestly ways, but ways which made an immediate appeal to the ordinary man. This brings us to another facet of Gandhi's genius, his power as a popular psychologist. He could not only dramatize himself; he could dramatize an issue with an unerring instinct. When others called meetings of protest against the Rowlatt bills [which gave British officials the right to hold Indians without charge and try them without jury] Gandhi called a *hartal* or religious strike. When he moved against the British government, it was not a tyranny against which one should fight, but a 'satanic' institution, with which no conscientious person could cooperate. When others walked out of the Assembly as a gesture of defiance, Gandhi walked sixty miles to the sea at Dandi to make illicit salt. In all that he did he not only brought the issue in question vividly before his constituents' minds, but contrived to make them feel morally superior to their physically stronger opponents. The load of supposed western superiority, moral as well as material, which had weighed so heavily on mid- and late-Victorian India was finally lifted and thrown back on the westerners themselves.

As a politician Gandhi's great work was to unite the masses with the classes in the national movement. He could persuade the masses to follow the classes because they believed him to be a good Hindu, a great soul; he could persuade the classes to accept his Hindu and, as many of them thought, his primitivist habits because it won them the masses. The industrialist put up with his hand-spinning, the politician with his loin-cloth, the epicure with his diet sheet, because they knew that these things won them the support they needed. They also knew that, when it came to dealing with the British, Gandhi could surpass them all, in argument, in tactics, and above all in making the British feel uncomfortable in their cherished field of moral rectitude. If Gokhale and Tilak and Bannerjea [all upper-class nationalist leaders] gave nationalism to the classes, the Mahatma gave a nation to the country.

The Village Storyteller Personifies Hindu Traditions

by R.K. Narayan

In the following selection, Nobel Prize–winning Indian author R.K. Narayan describes the persistence of Hindu beliefs in a rapidly changing world. To do so he uses the figure of a village storyteller and religious teacher, or pandit, a figure common in Indian rural life for centuries and even familiar in an increasingly technological and urbanized India. The storyteller not only carries religious knowledge from ancient texts such as the Vedas, he reminds Hindus of their traditions and responsibilities through the use of stories from the great epic *Ramayana*. He also personifies Hinduism by carrying on such rituals as fasting, bathing, and meditation.

Modern India is one of the largest nations on earth, with over a billion people, and even today most of its population lives in villages such as Narayan describes. He wrote the selection in 1964 when the nation was even more rural and less united by modern technological marvels such as satellites and cellular phones. Yet even then, with modernization on the march, Narayan suggests that the storyteller served as a constant link between Hinduism's present and past.

He is part and parcel of the Indian village community, which is somewhat isolated from the main stream of modern life. The nearest railway station is sixty miles away, to be reached by an occasional bus passing down the highway, which again may be an hour's marching distance from the village by a shortcut across the canal. Tucked away thus, the village consists of less than a hundred houses, scattered in six crisscross streets. The rice fields stretch away westward and merge into the wooded slopes of the mountains. Electricity is coming or has come to another village, only three miles away, and water is obtainable from a well open to the skies in the center of the village. All day the men and women are active in the fields, digging, ploughing, transplanting, or harvesting. At seven o'clock (or in the afternoon if a man-eater [tiger] is reported to be about) everyone is home.

Looking at them from outside, one may think that they lack the amenities of modern life; but actually they have no sense of missing much; on the contrary, they give an impression of living in a state of secret enchantment. The source of enchantment is the storyteller in their midst, a grand old man who seldom stirs from his ancestral home on the edge of the village, the orbit of his movements being the vegetable patch at the back and a few coconut palms in his front yard, except on some very special occasion calling for his priestly services in a village home. Sitting bolt upright, cross-legged on the cool clay-washed floor of his house, he may be seen any afternoon poring over a ponderous volume in the Sanskrit language mounted on a wooden reading stand, or tilting towards the sunlight at the doorway some old palm-leaf manuscript. When people want a story, at the end of their day's labours in the fields, they silently assemble in front of his home, especially on evenings when the moon shines through the coconut palms.

An Evening's Entertainment

On such occasions the storyteller will dress himself for the part by smearing sacred ash on his forehead and wrapping himself in a green shawl, while his helpers set up a framed picture of some god on a pedestal in the veranda, decorate it with jasmine garlands, and light incense to it. After these preparations, when the story-teller enters to seat himself in front of the lamps, he looks imperious and in complete control of the situation. He begins the session with a prayer, prolonging it until the others join and the valleys echo with the chants, drowning the cry of jackals. Time was when he narrated his stories to the accompaniment of musical instruments, but now he depends only on himself. "The films have taken away all the fiddlers and croon-ers, who have no time nowadays to stand at the back of an old storyteller, and fill his pauses with music," he often comments. But he can never really be handi-capped through the lack of an understudy or assistants, as he is completely self-reliant, knowing as he does by heart all the 24,000 stanzas of the *Ramayana*, the 100,000 stanzas of the *Mahabharata*, and the 18,000 stanzas of the *Bhagavata* [or Bhagavad Gita]. If he keeps a copy of the Sanskrit text open before him, it is more to demonstrate to his public that his narration is backed with authority.

The Pandit (as he is called) is a very ancient man, continuing in his habits and deportment the traditions of a thousand years, never dressing himself in more than two pieces of cotton drapery. (But sometimes he may display an amazing knowledge of modern life, acquired through the perusal of a bundle of old newspapers brought to him by the "weekly" postman every Thursday afternoon.) When he shaves his head (only on days prescribed in the almanac), he leaves just a small tuft on the top, since the ancient scriptures, the shastras, prescribe that a man should wear his hair no thicker than what could pass through the silver ring on his finger; and you may be sure he has on his finger a silver ring, because that is also prescribed in the shastras. Every detail of his life is set for him by what the shastras say; that is the reason why he finds it impossible to live in a modern town—to leave his home where his forefathers practiced unswervingly the codes set

Devout Hindus take part in ritual bathing and worshipping in the holy waters of the Baghmati River in front of the Pashupatinath Temple, the holiest Hindu temple in Nepal.

down in the shastras. He bathes twice daily at the well, and prays thrice, facing east or west according to the hour of the day; chooses his food according to the rules in the almanac, fasts totally one day every fortnight, breaking his fast with greens boiled in salt water. The hours that he does not spend in contemplation or worship are all devoted to study.

Maintaining Ancient Customs

His children could not, of course, accept his pattern of life and went their ways, seeking their livelihood in distant cities. He himself lives on the produce of his two acres and the coconut garden; and on the gifts that are brought him for storytelling—especially at the happy conclusion of a long series, or when God incarnates himself as a baby of this world or marries a goddess in the course of a story. He is completely at peace with himself and his surroundings. He has unquestioned faith in the validity of the *Vedas*, which he commenced learning when he was seven years old. It took him twelve years to master the intonation of the *Vedas*. He had also to acquire precise knowledge of Sanskrit grammar, syllabification, meaning of words.

Even his daily life is based on the authority of the *Vedas*, which have in them not only prayer and poetry, but also guidance in minor matters. For instance, whenever he finds his audience laughing too loudly and protractedly at his humour, he instantly quotes an epigram to show that laughter should be dignified and refreshing rather than demonstrative. He will openly admonish those who are seen scratching their heads, and quote authority to say that if the skin itches it should be borne until one can retire into privacy and there employ the tip of a stag-horn, rather than finger-nails, for the purpose. He has no doubt whatever that the *Vedas* were created out of the breath of God, and contain within them all that a man needs for his salvation at every level.

Eternal Truths, Different Forms

Even the legends and myths, as contained in the puranas, of which there are eighteen major ones, are mere illustrations of the moral and spiritual truths enunciated in the *Vedas*. "No one can understand the significance of any story in our mythology unless he is deeply versed in the *Vedas*," the storyteller often declares. Everything is interrelated. Stories, scriptures, ethics, philosophy, grammar, astrology, astronomy, semantics, mysticism, and moral codes—each forms part and parcel of a total life and is indispensable for the attainment of a four-square understanding of existence. Literature is not a branch of study to be placed in a separate compartment, for the edification only of scholars, but a comprehensive and artistic medium of expression to benefit the literate and the illiterate alike. A true literary composition should appeal in an infinite variety of ways; any set of stanzas of the *Ramayana* could be set to music and sung, narrated with dialogue and action and treated as the finest drama, studied analytically for an understanding of the subtleties of language and grammar, or distilled finely to yield esoteric truths.

The characters in the epics are prototypes and moulds in which humanity is cast, and remain valid for all time. Every story has implicit in it a philosophical or moral significance, and an underlining of the distinction between good and evil. To the storyteller and his audience the tales are so many chronicles of personalities who inhabited this world at some remote time, and whose lives are worth understanding, and hence form part of human history rather than fiction. In every story, since goodness triumphs in the end, there is no tragedy in the Greek sense; the curtain never comes down *finally* on corpses strewn about the stage. The sufferings of the meek and the saintly are temporary, even as the triumph of the demon is; everyone knows this. Everything is bound to come out right in the end; if not immediately, at least in a thousand or ten thousand years; if not in this world, at least in other worlds.

Over an enormous expanse of time and space events fall into proper perspective. There is suffering because of the need to work off certain consequences, arising from one's actions, in a series of births determined by the law of Karma. The strong man of evil continues to be reckless until he is destroyed by the tempo of his own misdeeds. Evil has in it, buried subtly, the infallible seeds of its own destruction. And however frightening a demon might seem, his doom is implied in his own evil propensities—a profoundly happy and sustaining philosophy which unfailingly appeals to our people, who never question, "How long, oh, how long, must we wait to see the downfall of evil?"

The Hindu Sense of Time

The events in Indian myths follow a calendar all their own, in which the reckoning is in thousands and tens of thousands of years, and actions range over several worlds, seen and unseen. Yet this immense measure of time and space does not add up to much when we view it against the larger timetable of creation and dissolution. Brahma, the four-faced god and Creator of the Universe, who rests on a bed of lotus petals in a state of contemplation, and by mere willing creates everything, has his own measure of night and day. In his waking half-day he creates the Universe, which passes through four well-defined epochs called *yugas*. Then Brahma falls asleep, and there is a total dissolution of everything. Brahma sleeps for twelve hours, wakes up, and the business of creation begins all over again and lasts another full cycle of four epochs.

Brahma's own life span is a hundred celestial years [3,600 human years], at the end of which he himself is dissolved, and nothing is left of creation or the Creator. The sun and the stars are put out and the oceans rise in gigantic waves and close over the earth. Ultimately even the waters from this deluge evaporate and are gone. A tremendous stillness, darkness, and vacuity occur. Beyond this cosmic upheaval stands a supreme God, who is untouched by time and change, and in whose reckoning creation and dissolution have occurred in the twinkling of an eye. He is the ultimate Godhead, called Narayana, Iswara, or Mahashakti. From this Timeless Being all activity, philosophy, scripture, stories, gods and demons, heroes and epochs, emanate, and in Him everything terminates.

One God in Many Forms

For certain purposes this Timeless Being descends to the practical plane in the form of a trinity of gods, Brahma, Vishnu, and Shiva, each of whom has his specific function. Brahma is the creator, Vishnu is the protector, and Shiva is the destroyer; and all of them have important roles in mythological stories, along with a host of minor gods (whom Indra heads) and an even larger host of evil powers broadly termed demon— *asuras* and *rakshasas;* added to these are the kings and sages of this earth. The pressures exerted by these different types of beings on each other, and their complex relationships at different levels, create the incidents and patterns of our stories.

The narratives may be taken to have come down to us mostly by word of mouth, at first, and were also recorded in the course of centuries. Each tale invariably starts off when an inquiring mind asks of an enlightened one a fundamental question. The substance of the story of the *Ramayana* was narrated by the sage Narada when Valmiki (who later composed the epic) asked, "Who is a perfect man?" Narada had heard the story from Brahma, and Brahma heard it from the Great God himself at a divine council. And so each tale goes back and further back to an ultimate narrator, who had, perhaps, been an eye-witness to the events. The report travels, like ripples expanding concentrically, until it reaches the storyteller in the village, by whom it is passed to the children at home, so that ninety per cent of the stories are known and appreciated and understood by every mortal in every home, whether literate or illiterate (the question does not arise).

Everyone knows what the hero achieves by God's grace, and also what the end of the demon is going to be. The tales have such inexhaustible vitality in them that people like to hear them narrated again and again, and no one has ever been known to remark in this country, "Stop! I've heard that one before." They are heard or read and pondered over again and again, engendering in the listener an ever-deepening understanding of life, death, and destiny.

A Refined Tradition of Love and Devotion in Danger

by Gita Mehta

Thanks to the rise of modern communications technology in such forms as satellite and cable television and the Internet, and thanks also to the lifting of certain economic restrictions in the 1990s, India is rapidly changing, becoming more modern in the Western and American sense. One effect of this is the rise of an educated, English-speaking, consumer-driven middle-class that some experts claim numbers at least 150 million. These changes are inevitably affecting Hindu customs and practices.

In the following selection author Gita Mehta revisits an eight-century-old Hindu poem, the *Gita Govinda*, in the context of these modern transformations. The *Gita Govinda* is a love song to the god Krishna, although this love is couched in often very romantic, even sensual language and imagery. Likewise the Jagannath Temple in the city of Puri in eastern India, where the *Gita Govinda* has been traditionally celebrated, is partly bedecked with erotic sculpture. Mehta worries that the divine love of Krishna symbolized by the *Gita Govinda* has been supplanted by a less refined understanding of love and eroticism. Gita Mehta is the author of three books concerned with the intersection of India and the

Western world: *Karma Cola, A River Sutra,* and *Snakes and Ladders.* She also wrote *Raj,* a historical novel set in India.

———————————

In the twelfth century the poet Jayadeva sang India's greatest love song outside the Jagannath Temple in the holy city of Puri so that passing strangers, forbidden entrance to the temple, could also listen to the trysts and deceptions, the separations and consummations, described in the *Gita Govinda.*

The Jagannath Temple is one of the holiest places of pilgrimage in India because it is home to the last benign incarnation of the god Vishnu. When this epoch is over, Vishnu will incarnate into Kalki and destroy the world.

In possession of such a valuable treasure, the priests of Jagannath are among the most ruthless in India. Only Hindus belonging to the higher castes may enter the temple. And yet Krishna, an earlier incarnation of Vishnu, is gained not by caste but by bhakti, the ecstatic love of the god felt by devotees who hope to die with his name on their lips. Pushing forward in the crush to touch the idol when the god is carried in procession through the streets of Puri, many devotees have been ground to death under the unstoppable momentum of the chariot's huge wooden wheels, giving the word "juggernaut" to the English language.

A Song of Love for Krishna

Now, standing before the Jagannath Temple where all could hear the *Gita Govinda,* Jayadeva sang of the milkmaid Radha's adoration for a beautiful young cowherd with a dark complexion and a perfect body, who plays haunting music on his flute and seduces every milk-maid, breaking Radha's heart even as he increases the intensity of her desire. The cowherd is the divine Krish-na, and in erotic images of breathtaking sensuality Radha makes love to Krishna in Jayadeva's *Song of God*.

There is a stone slab in the dusty ground in front of the temple to commemorate that moment when low-caste Hindus, Muslims, Buddhists, Jains, who could not enter the temple, all listened to Jayadeva sing of Radha's longing for the adulterous Krishna in some of the most sublime poetry ever written. They heard Radha's aching request to her companion to find this god who came to her bed marked with scratches from the embraces of other women, and the constant refrain of her shameless plea, "Oh friend, make him make love to me."

They listened to the sexual desire that made her es-cape home to wander through the dangerous jungles of the night to keep a tryst with the god who did not come and did not come while she waited in a fever of longing and fear, and when he finally appeared his body was streaked with another woman's collyrium and sandalwood paste, and he lied to her and still she trembled when he touched her.

Everyone who heard it became intoxicated by Jayadeva's ecstasy, even the listening king of Puri, who traditionally paid temple girls to perform devotional dances and songs in the temple precincts. Now the in-toxicated king decreed that the singers sing the *Gita Govinda* in the temple every day at dawn and at dusk. The lord had to be awakened by hearing this divine song. It had to be the last sound the god heard before he slept.

The love song spread through India like fire, adding

a new dimension to the mythology of Krishna. Indian history is full of these bhakti movements, great waves of spiritual ecstasy that break the hold of social and religious exclusion, to sweep every section of Indian society into the embrace of an all-inclusive passion. Poets and singers lost in their ecstatic songs have, century after century, mobilized millions of people to break the boundaries of social separation. But nowhere has bhakti been so perfectly stated as in the *Gita Govinda*, which Jayadeva sang in the holy city of Puri, expressing through Radha's lips his own longing for union with his god.

Modern Temple Visit

Eight centuries after Jayadeva sang his ecstasy to passing strangers, I went to the Jagannath Temple hoping to hear the temple singers sing his song when the god was put to sleep for the night, only to be told that the temple trust had been taken over by the government and there were no provisions for singers anymore.

Then a priest remembered that the last of the temple singers was still around. After many messages of entreaty she reluctantly agreed to come to the temple and sing the *Gita Govinda* a final time.

At eleven o'clock that night I entered the temple and made my way past the mighty tower with its circling erotic sculptures into the main hall. It was a warm evening and people were sitting on the ground talking to each other or prostrating themselves or telling their beads while children ran around with fresh flower garlands dangling from their fingers. Older people with austere features recited their mantras, holding in their laps leaves containing hibiscus and marigold blossoms and pieces of coconut as offerings to the god and his family. It was the usual combination of gregarious socializing and private worship that goes on in any Indian temple. At the back of the hall I found an old woman of about seventy years with a broken leg, lying full-length on her back, resting her head in her daughter's lap. The priest accompanying me whispered that this was the singer, but she was in such obvious discomfort I hesitated to disturb her and she acknowledged my greeting perfunctorily, turning her head away.

Hidden behind the huge doors that separated the inner sanctum from the main hall were the idols of the gods. While we waited for the doors to open, I sat on the ground watching the children crawling around their mothers on the stone floor and thought about the temple tower outside, with its sculptures locked in blissful copulation, wondering why Indians are able to look at these stone carvings without giggling but the most sophisticated Westerner, accustomed to pornographic television channels and sexually provocative advertisements, is overcome by self-consciousness. Was it the guiltless delight of the sculptures that made the visitor self-conscious?

A sudden clanging of bells interrupted my musings. The doors of the inner sanctum were flung open and the gods were revealed, wooden idols with totemic shapes from India's original tribal culture, which the new religions had not been able to subjugate, only to absorb.

In the presence of the gods the atmosphere in the hall became electric, charged with devotional intensity. People were singing and chanting prayers, their voices rising in a kind of urgency as they moved toward the railing that separated them from the sanctum. I saw the old temple singer limping forward.

The priests cleared a space in the crowd so that she could face the gods. Hands folded, eyes closed, she began to sing. Her voice was cracked and unmelodious. She could not manage the exacting rhythm, the precision of expression, the changing ragas conveying different moods, required by the *Gita Govinda*.

The priests quickly lost interest in her attempt to send the gods to bed with the sublime song soothing their dreams, and plunged the hall in darkness. The scent of burning camphor filled the hall. The old singer's voice petered out in confusion as the priests began circling the deities with their lamps and pressing food that had first been offered to the gods into the hands of the crowds mobbing them, swiftly seizing the money offered in exchange.

The old singer limped out of the hall, leaning on her daughter's shoulder, obviously irritated at my romantic fantasies, which had brought her out of the comfort of her home. As she grudgingly accepted the money I pressed into her fingers, I realized her irritation was justified.

Sublime Love No Longer

In the reality of modern India, Indian sexuality is increasingly dictated by Western fashion, and the sensual and sexual confidence that created India's majestic erotic monuments has now been replaced by packaged fantasies.

Young Indians, given access to MTV and its Easternized versions when India opened up to cable television in 1990, have begun styling themselves after the sexual and romantic practices of the mean streets of America or Europe, while lower down the ladder of wealth, where the social mores of traditional Indian society deny easy intercourse between the sexes until after marriages arranged by parents, proliferating publications suggest that the more urbanized the Indian, the more repressed his sexuality.

A new phenomenon is spreading from India's smallest towns to her largest cities—sex by advertisement. In the last two or three years there has been a steady increase in new magazines—with such names as *Broad-Minded* and *Pussy-Cat*—that carry articles on Mother Teresa next to pages and pages and pages of ads from all over India. . . .

We may be the land of the *Kama Sutra*, that great text on sexuality written by a celibate sage; we may have the Black Pagoda of Konarak with its twenty-foot-high statues locked in consummation; we may worship Shiva in his phallic form and place garlands on the yoni of the Goddess, but today we answer such advertisements as: *Well Educated Mature Hygiene-Conscious Couple Broad-Minded Fun-Loving, Interested to Meet Ladies, Men, Couples. Should Be Well Mannered, Decent. Strict Confy [confidence] Assured.* . . .

Come back, Jayadeva. India needs another *Gita Govinda*.

Can't you see the whole country is heaving, unfulfilled, telling strangers in magazines, "Oh friend, make him make love to me"?

New Forms of Caste Conflict

by Susan Bayly

In modern, democratic India, which has been independent since August 1947, the caste system is supposed to play no part in civil or legal life. In other words caste is to provide no basis for discrimination in such matters as the rule of law or property rights. Nevertheless, a modern state cannot legislate easily against long-held customs, especially those customs that are closely tied to religion, family, and community.

In the following selection historian Susan Bayly examines some of the ways in which caste is the source of conflict in modern India. One of these is the attempt by the Indian government to protect lower-caste Hindus, untouchables (or *Dalits*), or members of indigenous tribes by preserving government jobs and spots in universities for them. These measures have caused resentment in castes and social classes that had earlier been able to protect such privileges. They have also, in effect, reminded Indians of the importance of caste while ostensibly trying to limit its effects. Susan Bayly is a lecturer in history and social anthropology at the University of Cambridge.

———————

Susan Bayly, "'Caste Wars' and the Mandate of Violence," *The Cambridge History of India*. Cambridge, UK: The Cambridge University Press, 1999. Copyright © 1999 by Cambridge University Press. Reproduced by permission.

A . . . dimension of urban experience in recent years has been widespread fear and resentment of 'Mandalite' reservations schemes [which reserved places in universities and government jobs for low castes] among urban families with a long tradition of professional training and white-collar public employment. Often there are painful contradictions in these attitudes. Those concerned may be northern Kayasthas or Tamilnad Brahmans by birth, or others from the sort of service or commercial background that gave rise in past centuries to India's formerly compact and secure English-speaking intelligentsias. Since the 1970s these people have watched the growth and diversification of the Indian middle classes with considerable alarm. The expansion of trade and industry, and the commercialisation of agriculture, have greatly increased the numbers of families who can aspire to equip their sons and often their daughters with law, engineering or medical degrees, or with the qualifications to sit [take] the public service examinations.

The descendants of the old intelligentsias have been threatened on two fronts: by the new waves of ex-proprietary families who want their children to enter the universities and vocational colleges, and by members of thrusting 'peasant' groups and others of so-called Backward or Scheduled [either low-caste or untouchable] origin who are in a position to use the reservations system to achieve the same goal. This kind of urban English-speaking household will often have had no choice but to become acutely sensitive about the meaning of Kayastha, Khatri or Brahman birth for themselves and their children.

Whether justified or not, such people often fear that belonging to one of these 'Forward' [upper] castes or

It of the 'Manuvadi sys
s were unworthy]. On
k the opposing side, ob
aphic rape and reveng
nalist and screenwrite
1997 Roy's widely ac-
all Things, itself became
author's home state of
ging that the book's sex
class [south Indian] . . .
chable' household ser-
c morality.
tators who see trends
es (*gotras*) or the mar-
tions in middle-class
of caste itself, or of its
estigial ethnic identity
of 'true' caste. But . . .
many centuries exhib-
h in its more complex
ately ranked status cat-
merative forms which
external political and
the experiences of the
tended to reinforce
isparate but intercon-
be happening now is
etween matters of rit-
e broader and more
ised or ethnicity-like
estimony to the con-
generations of some-
e called caste, rather

'communities' may threaten or even negate their most cherished aspirations. During the 1990s, controversial court decisions and party political manoeuvres significantly reinforced these fears among members of these old cosmopolitan educated elites. The greatest blow here was the so-called 1992 Mandal judgement, in which the Indian Supreme Court upheld the principle of caste-based reservations in education and public service employment. This was followed by proposals from leaders of the Indian National Congress for an amendment to the Constitution introducing the principle of promotion quotas as well as recruitment reservations for members of the Scheduled Castes, Scheduled Tribes and OBC [other backward classes] groups. . . .

The Rise of "Casteism"

This persistence or reassertion of exclusive caste ties is all the more striking since in so many other ways the conventions of 'traditional' [caste] norms have been significantly eroded for people with this kind of background. . . . These trends have been most marked among educated English-speakers from the so-called Forward castes in Delhi and other major cities. Until recently this was a distinctive and confident world where the dominant voices were those of arts graduates and Indian Administrative Service 'batchmates' from the elite Delhi and Calcutta university colleges. These are people with family histories of public service and achievement in the liberal professions dating back to the pre-Independence [before 1947] period. Their forebears would normally include anglophone [English-speaking] jurists, educators and 'freedom fighters' who read reformist newspapers in the early twentieth century and took a leading role in early debates about Hindu nationhood and social '

In these urbane circles, the favoured lan
been 'secular', modernising and egalitarian, v
dency to disparage 'feudal' survivals in India
cluding the values and practices associa
'casteism'. These then are educated men an
who are caught by the same contradictions
in the Indian Constitution, striving to be 'mo
'casteless' in many areas of their personal liv
being forcibly reminded of the power of
tialised' or ethnicity-like [caste] allegiance:
wider world, by the militancy of organised 'D
touchables], and by alarming manifestations
war' in their troubled towns and rural hinter
some cases such people have expressed publi
thy for the Hindu supremacist cause on the
that its adherents' opposition to 'Mandalism'
for the nation than the recruitment of suppose
itless people to the universities and the public

At the same time, many prosperous Indian
ates in North America, western Europe and ,
have become keenly concerned with 'tradition
considerations. This is not surprising, given th
tainties of immigrant life and the advantag
gained even in ostensibly modern conditions
ing much of available 'community' networks.
ers of brides and grooms for their children,
class Indian expatriates (so-called NRIs, 'non-
Indians') may resemble English-speaking Indi
dwellers in stressing concern for income, ed
and astrological compatibility over the strict m
of [caste and subcaste]. This, however, may r
confident awareness that the successful comme
professional circles in which they move in L

an effective and timely indictme
tem' [believing that untouchabl
of the artists and literati who toc
jecting particularly to the film's ;
scenes, was the outspoken jou
Arundhati Roy. Ironically, in
claimed first novel, The God of Sr
the subject of legal action in th
Kerala, with the complainant all
scenes, which involve a middle
Christian woman and an 'unto
vant, represent a danger to publ

There are important comme
such as the merging of sub-cas
ginalisation of caste consider
marriages as a sign of the endin;
transformation into a form of v
without the power and meanin,
so-called caste Hindus have for
ited a consciousness of caste bo
manifestations as a grid of intric
egories and in these wider aggl
were so powerfully shaped by
economic changes. If anything,
post-Independence period hav
many manifestations of these
necting forms of caste. What ma
the emergence of a greater gulf
ual caste consciousness, and t
comprehensive forms of orgar
'community'. This, however, is
stant reinvention by different
thing which can still broadly
than to its disappearance.

Hinduism in the United States

by Gurinder Singh Mann, Paul David Numrich, and Raymond B. Williams

Hinduism is mostly associated with India and other nations in South Asia, yet over the last two centuries it has become a truly global religion. First, since India was part of the British Empire from 1757 to 1947, Hindus migrated, often as manual laborers, to places as far-flung as Kenya, South Africa, Trinidad, and Fiji. Even now, after the British Empire has mostly ceased to exist, large numbers of Hindus live in Britain and in other British Commonwealth nations such as Canada and Australia. In all these regions they continue to practice their faith.

Hinduism has become a common religion in the United States as well. This is largely an effect of changes in U.S. immigration law beginning in 1965. These changes made it possible for large numbers of people from developing countries to enter the United States and many Indian Hindus took advantage of the opportunity. The "first wave" of the late 1960s and 1970s consisted mostly of highly educated professionals who, along with their often now-grown-up children, remain prominent in such fields as medicine, engineering, and computers. People of other classes and educational backgrounds followed, and Indian Hindus have become a part of the patchwork of twenty-first-century America.

In the following selection, Gurinder Singh Mann, Paul David Numrich, and Raymond B. Williams examine some of the challenges facing Hindus in the United States. These range from the need to modify rituals and important rites of passage to generational conflicts with "Americanized" children. Throughout, the authors note that important beliefs not only remain intact but in many cases become even stronger among these so-called NRIs, or nonresident Indians.

As Dr. Ravindra Marri left his home in Bangalore, India, to enter a medical residency program at a hospital in New York City, his mother carefully handed him cloth-wrapped religious objects from their home shrine. They included a small image of Ganesh (the deity who protects people from danger and assists students), a copy of the *Bhagavad Gita* (a Hindu religious text), images of Krishna and Radha [an important god and goddess], a picture of the family's *guru* (religious teacher) in a silver frame, a small oil lamp, and an incense holder. In his New York apartment, Marri placed these objects on a shelf beside the bed. Later he went back to India to get married and returned to New York with his wife. She brought sacred objects from her home and set up a small shrine in the kitchen. They consolidated the sacred objects in a home shrine in the family room of their first house.

Because Hinduism is family oriented and home based, shrines in the home have a significant role. Most Hindu families have such shrines. Some are whole rooms set apart for elaborate shrine cabinets carved in

India. Others are as simple as a few pictures of deities and religious teachers on a wall or in a china closet. A considerable amount of Hindu religious life occurs in the home; the traditional marriage ceremony authorizes the husband and wife to perform religious rituals for the family. Indeed, the home shrine is an authentic residence of the gods and the site of most Hindu rituals, so it is possible to be an observant Hindu and rarely visit a temple. Some scholars say that Hinduism's secure place in domestic life, centered in home shrines and family rituals, is the main reason Hinduism has survived so successfully through the turbulent, centuries-long history of invasions and conquests of the Indian subcontinent. Its home-based strategy has also helped preserve Hinduism through the potentially unsettling process of immigration to the United States.

A home shrine is a statement of Hindu identity for a family, like a crucifix on the wall of a Roman Catholic home or prayer and Bible reading at the dinner table in a Protestant home. The parents' level of devotion determines the intensity of activity at the home shrine. Parents can select from a wide array of religious rituals represented in the various forms of Hinduism, and devotional activities have changed as the immigrant community has moved from the first to the second and then on to the third generation. . . .

Marking Life's Transitions

On important occasions when worshipers seek the favor of the gods, such as when moving into a new house or establishing a business, a Brahmin comes to the house to perform a special *Satya Narayan Puja*, a more elaborate *puja* [collection of rituals] featuring chants of sacred texts, offerings to the gods, and dedications of the parents and the home. Brahmins are members of the highest Indian caste; in the traditional social and religious ranking they are authorized to perform special rituals. In Brahmin households, the father can perform the rituals if he has been appropriately trained by his father, but others hire a Brahmin *pujari*, a priest who serves in a temple, or a Brahmin employed in another occupation who nonetheless knows the rituals and performs them for the Hindu community. Generally, the Brahmin must shorten the ritual and explain elements as he goes along in order to keep the attention of those who attend, especially the children of the second and third generations. At one ritual, for example, the children were surprised when the priests inserted into the traditional list of sacred rivers some familiar names of American rivers, reciting, "the Ganges, the Ohio, the Mississippi, and the Yamuna." A dinner, which makes the event a significant social occasion at which family and friends gather, follows the ceremony. It is common for Hindus in periods of transition from one stage of life to the next to make vows regarding career choices, family security, and the welfare and health of their children. They fulfill these vows by performing religious rituals or sponsoring readings of sacred texts in the home.

Important Ceremonies

Hindus have an elaborate series of 16 rituals to mark transitions, called *samskaras*, which begin before birth and continue after death with cremation and observances of the anniversary of death. Rarely, even in India, do families observe all these rituals. In the United States, the five rituals most often performed are those before birth, the name-giving for a newborn child, the sacred thread ceremony for Brahmin boys, marriage, and cremation.

Each ritual is adapted to the American context. For example, rituals performed during pregnancy are traditionally conducted in Sanskrit, a classical language of India and of the earliest Hindu sacred texts. Today, American Hindus announce this ritual in the same way that other Americans announce baby showers, and the rituals have taken on some aspects of the shower. In the same way, a Brahmin priest in the home performs the name-giving ceremony, but the surrounding social activities are similar to those for a Christian baptism. The sacred thread ceremony for a Brahmin boy occurs when he becomes a student. In earlier times in India, the boy would then leave home to live and study with a *guru.* Now the ceremony functions as a puberty ritual similar to a Christian confirmation or a Jewish bar mitzvah. During the ritual the boy receives a sacred thread. Afterward he wears it over his left shoulder as a symbol of his status as a Brahmin. Despite the Americanization of some aspects of the rituals in the United States, in many cases families return to India for some of the childhood rituals and for marriages so that these ceremonies can be performed according to traditional patterns and grandparents and the extended family can participate.

Because marriage marks a major transition of life into householder status, a wedding is the occasion for an elaborate ritual. Arranged marriage is the Indian tradition; many immigrants married their spouses in this way. Their parents selected their marriage partners and arranged the wedding. Hindus often remark that "the expectation in America is that you will marry the person you come to love; in India the expectation is that

you will love the one you marry." One young immigrant couple laughed together about their experience.
The man returned to India on a two-week vacation to
select a bride from among several girls his parents had
arranged for him to meet. Before he left New York, he
and some friends prepared a list of 10 questions he
would ask each girl at their first meeting. But when he
set eyes on one girl, he forgot the list because she was
so beautiful and nice—and "modern," with her hair cut
in a contemporary style. She was modern in her thinking, too; she said that she wanted to marry a pharma-
cist rather than a physician, because he would have
more time for his family. They married, and she joined
him in New York after obtaining her visa. They seem to
be very happily married.

Changing Views on Marriage and Dating

Because the Western custom of courtship and dating is
not part of the traditional pattern in India, many immigrant parents are reluctant to let their children date.
They are fearful of the results of romantic entangle-
ments and of possible casual sexual relations. Yet many
Hindu children born and raised in the United States re-
sist their parent's subtle attempts to select their spouses.
One family solved the problem of prom night by agreeing that their son could go to the prom, but only if
they chose the girl he invited. They then talked with
her parents to set the ground rules for the evening,
which put more emphasis on the evening than either
the boy or the girl desired. The evening was a success
from the parents' point of view, but both young people
were embarrassed and resented what they saw as artifi-
cial formality in the arrangement. They considered the

date to be a disaster and were glad when it was over.

Conflicts over dating and marriage illustrate a fundamental problem for Hindus in the United States. For parents, the primary emphasis of social relationships is on family and family ties, but for their American children it is on friendship. Dating can create tension, because parents see it as the first step toward starting a family, while young people simply want to enjoy and explore friendships and their feelings for one another. Increasingly, parents in the United States and even in India are agreeing to either "semiarranged marriages," in which the couple express interest in each other and ask their parents to negotiate a marriage, or "love marriages," in which the partners select each other—the pattern that many see as the American norm. It appears that so far, however, the divorce rate for Hindu immigrants is much lower than for the general American population.

A wedding is the Hindu ritual most likely to be witnessed by friends who are not Hindus. The typical ceremony includes a *homa* (fire sacrifice) during which a Brahmin priest pours oil, various grains, and offerings into a sacred fire while chanting the appropriate texts in Sanskrit from the *Vedas*, the most sacred ancient religious texts of India. Many priests now add explanations of the chants in English to help guests understand basic Hindu rituals and symbols. Such additions can point up the differences between tradition and the new circumstances of Hindus in the United States. In the middle of one ceremony, for example, the priest translated from Sanskrit into English the traditional roles of husband as provider and wife as homemaker. Then, looking up, he added wryly, "but now you are in America, so you will do whatever you want." Then he returned to the Sanskrit chant.

Most weddings are too large for homes. They are held in rented halls, with traditional elements sometimes adapted to meet new settings. One priest, for example, had to perform a symbolic *homa* sacrifice over a candle, because the local fire regulations in a Holiday Inn would not permit the full ritual to be carried out over an open fire. The bride generally wears a red *sari*—one long piece of fabric wound intricately around the body—threaded with gold and elaborate gold jewelry. A highlight of the wedding ceremony comes when the groom ties a thread around himself and his bride and they walk around the sacred fire seven times, repeating a traditional vow at each turn regarding food, strength, increasing wealth, good fortune, children, long life, and eternal friendship. Much gift-giving and a large banquet generally accompany wedding ceremonies in both India and the United States.

Marriage moves the couple into the traditional householder stage of life. Accordingly, the priest urges them to establish themselves securely in regard to worldly goods and to provide well for their children. These social obligations will be their responsibility until the children are educated and established in homes of their own. Then, according to the traditional pattern, the parents will enter the third stage of life, gradual separation from the responsibilities of the householder. A few then enter the fourth and final stage, becoming *sannyasin*, people who separate themselves from all worldly attachments to pursue lives of simplicity and spiritual devotion. Few Hindu immigrants in the post-1965 [immigration] wave have reached retirement age, and only a few parents of immigrants have become permanent residents of the United States. Even fewer have entered the traditional fourth stage and given up all social obligations or ties. However, some immigrants do commit themselves to full-time volunteer service in Hindu temples and organizations following retirement. . . .

The Lasting Importance of Classic Texts

The chants used in [many] family rituals are from the *Rig Veda*, the most sacred Hindu scripture. This collection of hymns is the world's oldest sacred scripture still used in worship today. Although only a few worshipers understand the Sanskrit language in which the hymns are written, they value the rhythm and power of the chanting. Hindus in the United States circulate audio-cassettes of Vedic chanting, and some chants are available on the Internet.

A young Brahmin named Rajgopal Krishnacharya memorized the Sanskrit verses of the *Vedas* by repeating them with his father every morning at the family *puja* as he was growing up in India. Now he is an engineer living in Oklahoma and is one of the few people there who know the chants. He is often invited to lead rituals in Hindu homes in the area. Some of the chants have slipped from his memory, so he collects copies of the texts that include pronunciations of the Sanskrit words to refresh his memory and make him able to chant correctly.

Hindu homes are more than the primary sites of religious teaching, rituals, and ceremonies. In the years before American Hindus established temples and cultural centers, homes were the gathering places for religious groups. Relatives and friends began to gather in homes once or twice a month on the weekend for worship, study, or meditation. Through these groups, Hindus could pursue the four traditional paths of Hindu practice: *bhakti* (devotion), *yoga* (meditation), *jnana* (knowledge), and *karma* (action).

Special Practices

Devotional groups gather before images of deities or other sacred objects to express their reverence. A common form of expression in devotion is to sing sacred hymns and songs in honor of the deity or sacred person. These hymns, or *bhajans*, are in the regional languages of India, such as Gujarati, Hindi, Tamil, Telugu, and Malayalam. They take on a distinct ethnic identity.

Meditation groups focus on the physical, mental, and spiritual disciplines of *yoga*. They have spread some of the Indian ideas and practices that have significantly influenced American society. However, while many Americans have adopted some elements of Hindu meditation and other Hindu-influenced practices such as vegetarianism, surprisingly few Hindu immigrants practice yoga.

Followers of the *jnana* path meet in homes to engage in detailed study of Hindu religious texts. Study groups called *Gita mandals* (*mandals* meaning "society") have met in homes for years to study the *Bhagavad Gita*, the best-loved and best-known Hindu religious text. It consists of a philosophical and devotional dialogue between a warrior named Arjuna and his charioteer, who is really the god Krishna. The poetic dialogue takes place on a battlefield just before a battle between two royal families. It contains Hinduism's basic teachings about the gods, duty, devotion, and many other aspects of the Hindu worldview. The *Gita* has become a religious classic because, over the centuries, teachers have been able to interpret its enigmatic verses in ways that are meaningful to Hindus living in many times and places. Now they are applying its lessons to the new and different lives that Hindus are leading in the United States. . . .

The paths of devotion, meditation, and study are not mutually exclusive, and Hindus generally forge creative combinations of all three as they attempt to create a style of worship and religious practice appropriate to their new homeland and surroundings. Hindu immigrants also grapple with the age-old question: What is the better way to preserve religious traditions and transmit them to one's children, through ritual or word? Is it better to follow traditional rituals using the sacred Sanskrit language and the gestures that have always accompanied the language? Perhaps the beauty and power of the repeated chants and actions will attract the loyalty and allegiance both of immigrants and their children. Or is it better to rely on words to communicate, interpreting the sacred teachings to give children a clear understanding of the intellectual foundation of their beliefs and practices? Perhaps transmitting basic teachings to children and grandchildren, usually in English, will establish the foundation of a truly American Hinduism. One form of communication that offers a compromise is visual presentation of sacred Hindu stories through acting and reciting.

Hindu Texts in Modern Forms

Several sacred texts lend themselves well to performance, spoken recitation, and teaching. Two ancient epics are particularly popular in both India and the

United States. The *Ramayana* is the story of good King Rama, whose beautiful wife, Sita, is kidnapped by evil King Ravana. (Rama is a Hindu god, and Sita is his companion goddess.) In the long search for Sita, Rama is aided by his brother, Lakshmana, and by Hanuman, the king of the monkeys. Finally, after many heroic deeds and much soul-searching, they rescue Sita from the island of Sri Lanka, off the southeastern coast of India. The story has long been popular not only in India but throughout Southeast Asia and in other countries where Hindus have carried their culture. A dramatization of the *Ramayana* shown as a serial on the Indian government television network over several weeks became the most popular television show in India. Throughout the United States, Indian video outlets and grocery stores distribute copies of this show. Hindus watch them as entertainment in their homes and as teaching in religious gatherings.

The other popular ancient epic is the *Mahabharata*, the story of a great war between two clans of cousins, the good Pandavas and the bad Kauravas. The complex story of the Pandavas' effort to regain territory they lost to the Kauravas is the world's longest epic poem, complete with exciting tales, theological reflections, intrigue, a long love story, examples of moral behavior, and philosophical musings. The *Bhagavad Gita* is only a small section of the *Mahabharata*, inserted into the long story at the point of the decisive battle. Arjuna, the hero of the Pandavas, sees his cousins arrayed on the opposite side of the battlefield, throws his bow and arrows to the side, and sits down in his chariot. The question that begins the dialogue with Krishna is whether he should enter into battle and kill his cousins. The surprising answer leads to a long discus-sion about duty, the goals of life, and the role of faithfulness and devotion in gaining liberation from the cycles of birth and death. Like the *Ramayana*, the *Mahabharata* was made into a long-running series on Indian television.

Videotapes are used to retell the story in America. In addition, young people use dance and dramatic acting to perform episodes from both stories at religious and cultural gatherings. Other Hindu sacred texts, called *puranas*, contain the stories of the Hindu gods. Some are in Sanskrit and are accepted as sacred texts by all Hindus. Other texts, most of them in the more widely used regional languages, come from the subdivisions of Hinduism and are used only by Hindus who worship a particular deity or follow a certain saint or *guru*. . . .

Keeping Traditions Alive for "Americanized" Children

Immigrant parents are often anxious to start religious groups when their children become old enough to enter school and begin to be shaped by influences outside the home. At that time the parents tend to seek people from the same religious tradition to help them raise their children in ways that will preserve their values, identity, and relationships with their Hindu heritage. Groups of Hindu parents in several cities have started Sunday schools similar to those in Christian churches in order to teach their children the basics of Hinduism and Indian culture. These met at first in homes, then in rented halls or in the cultural centers that sprang up when the Asian Indian community grew large enough to support them. At these Sunday schools, children learned the basic rituals, religious stories and teachings, and symbolic religious art and drama.

Summer camps and retreats for children and young people supplement the Sunday schools. These camps are intended to help parents convey Hinduism to their children and, in doing so, to preserve, protect, and pass on the spiritual heritage of India. One of the first summer camps was held in the Pocono Mountains at a retreat center led by an American woman who converted to Hinduism and became a religious teacher for families of immigrants. Another way Hindu parents can attempt to immerse their children in their religion and in Indian culture is to take or send them back to India for visits to relatives and sacred shrines and for instruction by religious leaders. Hindus in India commonly go on pilgrimages to noted temples, such as the Krishna temple at Dwarka in Gujarat or the Venkateswara temple in Andhra Pradesh, in the southeast. They also visit sacred sites, such as the Ganges River, or holy persons. Visits to India by American Hindus take on aspects of sacred pilgrimages. Religious groups organize some tours, but families privately conduct most visits.

As children of the second generation reach college age, they begin to learn about Hinduism and Indian culture in courses at colleges and universities. In previous decades these courses existed to teach U.S. college students about distant cultures and religions. Now an increasing number of students in the courses are Hindus who want to learn more about their own religion. One reason the function of the courses has changed in recent years is that the affluent immigrant community has been active in raising funds for programs in Indian studies at major universities such as Columbia, the University of California at Santa Barbara, and Indiana University.

The family remains, however, the primary vehicle through which Hindu traditions pass from one generation to the next. It is also the setting within which individuals form their own religious identities. In the United States, Hindu families must meet these responsibilities without the wide support network that exists in Indian society. And it is hard. One mother remarked, "Here I have to be priest and preacher, and it doesn't work."

Many parents say that they have found themselves to be more religious in the United States than they were in India, partly because they have to organize all religious functions themselves and to provide all religious instruction for their children. When speaking about themselves, the immigrants describe the purpose of religious activities as "to gain peace," "to show devotion to God" and "to gain God's blessing." When they speak about the purpose of religion for their children and grandchildren, they respond, "so they will know who they are," "so they will not get lost in American society," and "so my son will have the best of both cultures."

Glossary

absolutist school: A school of Hindu philosophy emphasizing the oneness of all gods and creation.

Agni: A Vedic god of fire.

Arjuna: A Kshatriya-caste warrior and human hero of the Bhagavad Gita.

Atman: The individual self or soul.

avatar: An incarnation of a higher god.

Bhagavad Gita: The Song of the Lord, one of the central Hindu texts.

bhakti: Personal devotion.

Brahma: The creator god.

Brahman: The ultimate godhead; divine reality.

Brahman/Brahmin: The highest, or priestly, caste.

Buddhism: A major world religion emerging out of Hinduism during the sixth century B.C.

deva: A god.

devi: A goddess.

dharma: Duty or teaching.

Durga: A mother and warrior goddess.

Ganesha: An elephant-headed god and remover of obstacles; son of Shiva and Parvati.

guru: Teacher

Hanuman: A monkey god featured in the *Ramayana* and prized for his loyalty and courage.

Indra: A Vedic god of war.

Islam: A monotheistic faith emerging out of Arabia during the seventh century; later the second-largest religion in India.

Jainism: An offshoot of Hinduism dating from the sixth century B.C. and emphasizing nonviolence and personal devotion.

jati: Subcaste

Kali: A mother goddess often associated with the taking and giving of life.

kama: Pleasure.

karma: Action; also the consequences of past actions.

Krishna: A popular Hindu god depicted as a cowherd and, in the Bhagavad Gita, a charioteer; an avatar of Vishnu.

Kshatriya: The second-highest, or warrior, caste.

Lakshmi: A goddess of good fortune and wife of Vishnu.

Laws of Manu: A Hindu text concerned with daily life, ethics, and morality.

lingam: A phallic symbol used in the worship of Shiva.

Mahabharata: An epic poem of ancient India and early Hinduism.

mantra: A verbal prayer, often a pattern of repeated Sanskrit words.

maya: Illusion; the world.

moksha: The release from the cycle of death and reincarnation; the goal of most Hindus.

pandit: A teacher or sage.

Parvati: A goddess and consort of Shiva.

puja: Personalized worship, often in the form of devotion and offerings to a particular god or goddess.

Puranas: Hindu texts concerned with the lives of gods and goddesses.

Purusha: The original "Person" sacrificed to create humanity and the caste system.

Radha: A goddess and consort of Krishna.

Rama: A god revered as the ideal king and husband; hero of the *Ramayana;* an avatar of Vishnu.

Ramayana: An epic poem concerned with the exploits and challenges faced by Rama and Sita; known in many versions in India and Southeast Asia.

Rig-Veda: The earliest Hindu text.

rishi: A Vedic sage or teacher.

samsara: The wheel of birth, death, and rebirth; a reference to the process of reincarnation.

sannyasi: A Hindu believer who has renounced the world and all attachments.

Sanskrit: A Hindu religious language.

Saraswati: A goddess of knowledge.

Shaivism: Devotion to Shiva.

shakti: The female side of cosmic power.

shastra: A guidebook; educational text.

Shiva: One of three great Hindu gods; the lord of the dance (cosmic energy); the creator and destroyer of life.

Shudra/Sudra: The lowest, or laboring, caste.

Sita: A consort of Rama, considered the ideal wife.

sutra: An educational text.

theistic school: A school of Hinduism focusing on the worship and attributes of a specific god, usually Shiva or Vishnu.

untouchables: The popular name for the "outcastes" who performed the most menial jobs; they are more generally known today as *dalits* or, following Mahatma Gandhi, *harijans*, meaning "children of God."

Upanishads: Means "Sitting near a teacher"; early Hindu texts focusing on lessons between a guru and his students.

Vaishnavism: Devotion to Vishnu.

Vaisya: The third-highest, or productive, caste: craftspeople, cultivators, and shopkeepers.

varna: Color or caste.

Vedanta: A school of Hindu philosophy emphasizing the "end of the Vedas."

Vedas: Books of Knowledge; the oldest Hindu texts.

Vishnu: One of the three great Hindu gods; the preserver of life.

yoga: A school of Hinduism emphasizing the discipline of focusing and concentrating in order to attain *moksha*.

Chronology

B.C.
2800–1800
Span of the Indus Valley civilization, thought by some to feature early Hindu rites, such as meditation and ritual bathing as well as early versions of Shiva and of Devi-mata, a mother goddess.

1500
Indo-Aryans begin migrating into India. Migrations continue for over one thousand years, until migrants go as far as southern India and Sri Lanka.

1200
The Rig-Veda, the earliest Hindu text, is composed.

1100–200
Other important Hindu texts, such as the other Vedas and the Upanishads, are composed.

490–410
The life of Siddhartha Gautama, the founder of Buddhism; some Hindus consider him to be an avatar of the god Vishnu.

400 B.C.–A.D. 400
The *Mahabharata*, including the section known as the Bhagavad Gita, is composed.

200 B.C.–A.D. 200
The *Ramayana* is composed.

A.D.
150–500
The Laws of Manu and other important texts concerned with Hindu ethics are composed.

200–800
Hindus migrate to Southeast Asia.

500–900
Bhakti, or devotional, poets flourish in southern India.

788–820
The life of Shankara, a Hindu philosopher of the absolutist school.

1017–1137
The life of Ramanuja, a Hindu philosopher of the theistic school.

1000
Muslims begin invading and migrating into India.

1211–1526
The Islamic Delhi Sultanate controls much of northern and central India.

1440–1518
The life of Kabir, a bhakti poet who sought a middle path between Hinduism and Islam.

1469–1539
The life of Guru Nanak, the founder of Sikhism.

1498
The Portuguese arrive in India to set up trading posts and seek Christian converts.

1526
The Islamic Mogul Empire is established.

1600
The English East India Company is founded. Its first permanent trading post is established at Surat in western India in 1615.

1707
Aurangzeb, the last great Mogul emperor dies.

1757
The English East India Company takes control of the northeastern Indian province of Bengal; Britain becomes the dominant power in India, replacing the Moguls.

1772–1883
The life of Hindu reformer Ram Mohan Roy.

1828
The Brahmo Samaj Society, designed to formulate a Hindu response to the challenge represented by the British, is founded.

1836–1886
The life of Ramakrishna, who did much to introduce Hinduism to the Western world.

1838
The British begin to transplant Indian laborers to such parts of the British Empire as the Caribbean, East Africa, and Fiji.

1858

After the Sepoy Rebellion of the previous year, the British government takes direct control of India and soon dissolves the East India Company.

1863–1902

The life of Vivekenanda, the advocate of Vedanta, the philosophy of "the end of the Vedas."

1869–1948

The life of Mahatma Gandhi.

1885

The Indian National Congress, or Congress Party, which is to lead the Indian independence movement, is founded.

1891–1956

The life of B.R. Ambedkar, an advocate of the rights and protections of India's untouchables.

1905

The Arya Samaj, an organization seeking a Hindu path to independence, is founded.

1930

Gandhi stages his Salt March, a nonviolent protest against unfair British laws. It helps turn him into a figure of global fame.

1947

India becomes independent, although partitioned into two nations: mostly Hindu India and mostly Muslim Pakistan. Sectarian riots among Hindus, Muslims, and Sikhs kill hundreds of thousands.

1950

Indians begin migrating to rich Western nations.

1955

India's parliament passes the Untouchability Offences Act, which establishes penalties for caste discrimination. Later laws will establish quotas in political bodies, government jobs, and places in universities for untouchables. In the face of many objections and challenges, these measures will be upheld by the 1992 Mandal Commission.

1965

New American immigration laws permit large numbers of Indians to enter the United States. The first Hindu temples in the United States are built in the early 1970s.

1966

The International Center for Krishna Consciousness is founded in Los Angeles. Along with the interest in Hindu ideas of Western pop stars like the Beatles, it raises awareness of the faith in North America.

1971

East Pakistan becomes independent as Bangladesh after a war between India and Pakistan.

1982

The Bharaitiya Janata Party (BJP), or Indian People's Party, is founded. Growing out of earlier Hindu nationalist movements, it seeks political power at the national level.

1990s

Indian immigrants play a major role in the development of high-technology businesses in the United States; the city of Bangalore in southern India becomes a global high-tech center.

1992

After Hindu extremists destroy a mosque in the city of Ayodha, considered the birthplace of the god Rama, sectarian riots between Hindus and Muslims break out.

1997

K.R. Narayanan becomes the first untouchable president of India, a largely ceremonial but symbolically important post.

1998

The BJP becomes the ruling party in India, having attracted much support from high-caste Hindus concerned over the growing power of the lower castes and the untouchables. Both India and Pakistan become official nuclear powers.

2004

The BJP is dealt a surprise blow: In national elections it is soundly defeated by a revived Congress Party representing liberal and secular ideals.

For Further Research

Books

Bridget Allchin and Raymond Allchin, *The Birth of Indian Civilization.* New York: Penguin, 1968.

A.L. Basham, ed., *A Cultural History of India.* London: Oxford University Press, 1975.

Susan Bayly, *Caste, Society, and Politics in India from the Eighteenth Century to the Modern Age.* The New Cambridge History of India IV:3. Cambridge, UK: Cambridge University Press, 1999.

Nirad Chaudhuri, *Hinduism: A Religion to Live By.* New York: Oxford University Press, 1979.

Wendy Doniger and Brian K. Smith, trans., *Laws of Manu.* New York: Penguin, 1991.

Ainsley T. Embree, ed., *Sources of Indian Tradition.* New York: Columbia University Press, 1988.

Eliza Fay, *Original Letters from India.* London: Hogarth, 1986.

John Y. Fenton et al., *Religions of Asia.* New York: St. Martin's, 1983.

Gavin Flood, *An Introduction to Hinduism.* Cambridge, UK: Cambridge University Press, 1996.

Christopher Fuller, *The Camphor Flame: Popular Hinduism and Society in India.* Princeton, NJ: Princeton University Press, 1992.

Mohandas K. Gandhi, *The Gandhi Reader.* Ed. Homer A. Jack. Bloomington: Indiana University Press, 1956.

Ian Grant, *Bali: Morning of the World.* Rutland, VT: Charles E. Tuttle, 1969.

René Grousset, *The Civilization of India.* New York: Tudor, 1931.

Waldemar Hansen, *The Peacock Throne.* New York: Holt, Rinehart and Winston, 1972.

Andrew Harvey, ed., *Teachings of the Hindu Mystics.* Boston: Shambala, 2001.

John Stratton Hawley, *Songs of the Saints of India.* New York: Oxford University Press, 1988.

John Keay, *India: A History.* New York: Atlantic Monthly, 2000.

David M. Knipe, *Hinduism: Experiments in the Sacred.* San Francisco: HarperCollins, 1991.

Kim Knott, *Hinduism: A Very Short Introduction.* New York: Oxford University Press, 1998.

Gurinder Singh Mann, Paul David Numrich, and Raymond B. Williams, *Buddhists, Hindus, and Sikhs in America.* New York: Oxford University Press, 2001.

P.J. Marshall, *The British Discovery of Hinduism in the Eighteenth Century.* Cambridge, UK: Cambridge University Press, 1970.

Gita Mehta, *Karma Cola.* New York: Vintage International, 1979.

———, *Snakes and Ladders.* New York: Talese/Doubleday, 1997.

Ramesh Menon, *The Ramayana.* New York: North Point, 2003.

Barbara Stoler Miller, trans., *The Bhagavad-Gita: Krishna's*

Counsel in Time of War. New York: Columbia University Press, 1986.

——, *Love Song of the Dark Lord: Jayadeva's "Gota Govinda."* New York: Columbia University Press, 1977.

R.K. Narayan, *Gods, Demons, and Others.* New York: Viking, 1967.

——, *The Mahabharata: A Shortened Prose Version of the Indian Epic.* New York: Viking, 1978.

Wendy Doniger O'Flaherty, ed., *Textual Sources for the Study of Hinduism.* Manchester, UK: Manchester University Press, 1988.

Jeffery Paine, *Father India.* New York: HarperCollins, 1998.

Sarvepalli Radhakrishnan and Charles A. Moore, eds., *A Sourcebook in Indian Philosophy.* Princeton, NJ: Princeton University Press, 1967.

Glyn Richards, ed., *A Sourcebook of Modern Hinduism.* London: Curzon, 1985.

Paul William Roberts, *Empire of the Soul.* New York: Riverhead, 1994.

Arvind Sharma, *Hinduism for Our Times.* New York: Oxford University Press, 1996.

Khushwant Singh, *Train to Pakistan.* New York: Grove, 1956.

Percival Spear, *A History of India.* Vol. 2. Middlesex, England: Penguin, 1965.

Romila Thapar, *A History of India.* Vol. 1. Baltimore: Penguin, 1966.

Peter Van der Veer, *Religious Nationalism: Hindus and Muslims in India.* Berkeley and Los Angeles: University of California Press, 1994.

Raymond Brady Williams, ed., *A Sacred Thread: Modern Transmission of Hindu Traditions in India and Abroad.* Chambersburg, PA: Anima, 1992.

Stanley Wolpert, *A New History of India.* New York: Oxford University Press, 1997.

Web Sites

About Hinduism, www.hinduism.about.com. This Web site provides a broad overview of Hinduism both past and present as well as links to articles on specific Hindu-related topics. It is part of the general informational service, about.com.

Hinduism Today, www.hinduismtoday.com. This Web site is the online version of a Hindu news magazine published since 1979. The site's focus is on modern rather than historical Hinduism. It contains articles and links on many topics intended for both Hindus and those interested in the subject and has a very useful search function.

The Hindu Universe, www.hindunet.org. This Web site is managed by an organization known as Global Hindu Electronic Networks and its homepage provides links to articles on such topics as the history of Hinduism, Hindu customs, and contemporary issues in Hinduism.

Hindu Web site, www.hinduwebsite.com. This is a very thorough Web site designed to reinforce knowledge of Hindu traditions and customs among believers today. The homepage provides links to general articles on such subjects as Hindu scripture and relations between Hinduism and other faiths.

Index